# Cambridge Elements ≡

**Elements in Applied Evolutionary Science**
edited by
David F. Bjorklund
*Florida Atlantic University*

# THE EVOLVED MIND AND MODERN EDUCATION: STATUS OF EVOLUTIONARY EDUCATIONAL PSYCHOLOGY

David C. Geary
*University of Missouri*

 THE EVOLUTION INSTITUTE

CAMBRIDGE
UNIVERSITY PRESS

Shaftesbury Road, Cambridge CB2 8EA, United Kingdom

One Liberty Plaza, 20th Floor, New York, NY 10006, USA

477 Williamstown Road, Port Melbourne, VIC 3207, Australia

314–321, 3rd Floor, Plot 3, Splendor Forum, Jasola District Centre,
New Delhi – 110025, India

103 Penang Road, #05–06/07, Visioncrest Commercial, Singapore 238467

Cambridge University Press is part of Cambridge University Press & Assessment,
a department of the University of Cambridge.

We share the University's mission to contribute to society through the pursuit of
education, learning and research at the highest international levels of excellence.

www.cambridge.org
Information on this title: www.cambridge.org/9781009454841

DOI: 10.1017/9781009454858

When citing this work, please include a reference to the DOI 10.1017/9781009454858

First published 2024

*A catalogue record for this publication is available from the British Library.*

ISBN 978-1-009-45484-1 Hardback
ISBN 978-1-009-45481-0 Paperback
ISSN 2752-9428 (online)
ISSN 2752-941X (print)

# The Evolved Mind and Modern Education

## Status of Evolutionary Educational Psychology

### Elements in Applied Evolutionary Science

DOI: 10.1017/9781009454858
First published online: February 2024

David C. Geary
*University of Missouri*

**Author for correspondence:** David C. Geary, gearyd@missouri.edu

**Abstract:** Humans have an extraordinary ability to create evolutionarily novel knowledge, such as writing systems and mathematics. This accumulated knowledge over several millennia supports large, dynamic societies that now require children to learn this novel knowledge in educational settings. This Element provides a framework for understanding the evolution of the brain systems that enable innovation and novel learning and how these systems can act on human cognitive universals, such as language, to create evolutionarily novel abilities, such as reading and writing. Critical features of these networks include the top–down control of attention, which is central to the formation of evolutionarily novel abilities, as well as self-awareness and mental time travel that support academic self-concepts and the generation of long-term educational goals. The basics of this framework are reviewed and updated here, as are implications for instructional practices.

**Keywords:** evolutionary educational psychology, academic learning, brain and cognitive evolution, instructional approaches, cumulative culture

ISBNs: 9781009454841 (HB), 9781009454810 (PB), 9781009454858 (OC)
ISSNs: 2752-9428 (online), 2752-941X (print)

# Contents

## 1 Introduction

More than ever, success in the modern world requires a formal education in a variety of academic domains, such as mathematics. Academic competencies at the end of schooling influence employability, wages, and the ability to navigate the complexities of living in a developed economy (Richmond-Rakerd et al., 2020; Ritchie & Bates, 2013). Thus, it is not surprising that complex educational systems have emerged and expanded in response to increases in the social and economic complexity of societies (Goldin, 1999; F. O. Ramirez & Boli, 1987). The spread of schools and the expectation that all children will receive an extended formal education belie the deeper question of why schooling is necessary. After all, most young children acquire many complex competencies, such as language, without any type of formal or informal (e.g., parental tutoring) education. Why can most preschoolers learn the complexities of their native language by simply engaging in everyday social activities, but several years later struggle to decode (sound out) unfamiliar words during the act of reading? These differences in the ease of learning can be linked to the evolutionary history of the competency (Geary, 1995).

Language and other social competencies are human universals, and the basic brain and cognitive systems that guide their development are in place early in life. For instance, the basic neural architecture of the language system forms prenatally (Keunen et al., 2017), and brain imaging studies confirm its specialization for language in the first months of life (Dehaene-Lambertz et al., 2010). The universality, inherent brain architecture, and structure in the developmental elaboration of language skills (Brown, 1973) suggest it was present with the emergence of *Homo sapiens* at least 200,000 years ago (Bae et al., 2017; Pinker & Bloom, 1990). Other social competencies, such as sensitivity to social cues (e.g., based on body posture), are common among primates, suggesting the basic architecture of these abilities emerged at least 25 million years ago (Christov-Moore et al., 2014). The basic structure of the hippocampus evolved in vertebrates more than 500 million years ago and enables the formation of cognitive representations of the physical world that support navigation and related spatial abilities (Broglio et al., 2015; E. A. Murray et al., 2018).

Now, contrast these evolutionary histories with the historical emergence of academic domains and schooling. Formal instruction, as we might recognize it today, first appeared about 5,000 years ago with the emergence of large complex societies (Eskelson, 2020). Education in these contexts was typically limited to a small number of scribes whose literacy and numeracy training was used to support the bureaucratic management of these societies. The expansion of schooling was slow, and fitful. Universal education emerged across many parts of Europe over the past 400 years (Goldin, 1999; F. O. Ramirez & Boli, 1987). In many areas of the Western world, universal education was not achieved until well into the nineteenth century and sometimes the early twentieth and remains to be achieved in some parts of the world today (Golden, 1999).

There is evidence for recent evolutionary selection for traits (e.g., general ability, conscientiousness) that influence educational attainment (Srinivasan et al., 2018) and examples of how investment in education can result in reproductive benefits (e.g., more grandchildren) (Galor & Klemp, 2019). Nevertheless, the recency and the historical selectivity of educational opportunities make it unlikely that the same types of brain and cognitive scaffolds that evolved to support abilities with deep evolutionary histories, such as language and spatial abilities, are as elaborated or as universally available to support academic learning.

Consideration of the evolutionary history of cognitive abilities has profound implications for our understanding of children's cognitive development and their academic learning (Geary, 2007, 2008; Sweller et al., 2019). Universal competencies with a deep history are termed biologically primary abilities or folk abilities, whereas those that are cultural inventions are termed biologically secondary abilities to emphasize they are built from primary ones largely through instruction in school (Geary, 1995). In the next section, I provide a brief overview of brain and cognitive evolution and provide a taxonomy of primary abilities and a model of how they are elaborated and adapted to local conditions during development. The section includes brief overviews of the cognitive systems that contribute to learning and innovation. The third section focuses on secondary abilities and formal schooling broadly, the fourth explores noncognitive contributions to educational outcomes, and the fifth addresses instructional implications. The core foci of each section are shown in Table 1.

## 2 Brain and Cognitive Evolution

Even Wallace, the codiscoverer of natural selection, argued that the human mind differed from other minds, having qualities that cannot be explained by evolutionary processes (Wallace, 1869). The human brain and mind do differ in some significant ways from those of other minds (Penn et al., 2008), but these differences do not mean it has eluded the crucible of evolutionary selection (Geary, 2005). There are many features of the human brain and associated cognitive abilities that are evolutionarily conserved, that is, the same basic systems are found in other primates (Smaers & Vanier, 2019), mammals (Assaf et al., 2020), and, as mentioned, sometimes across all vertebrates (E. A. Murray et al., 2018). Differences across species generally reflect

**Table 1** Outline of evolutionary and cultural changes resulting in modern education.

**Brain and Cognitive Evolution**

The goal is to provide an overview of constraint and plasticity in brain and cognition and their evolution. This sets the foundation for understanding the uniquely human ability to innovate and create evolutionarily novel knowledge and ultimately to learn this knowledge in school settings.

**Biologically Primary or Evolved Folk Domains**

Universal forms of human cognition, such as language, are described. The basic structure of these abilities are inherent and form prenatally or early postnatally, but many are plastic and become refined and adapted to local conditions through children's engagement in species typical experience-expectant behaviors, such as social play. Plasticity in individual brain areas and networks of areas opens the possibility (within limits) of modifying these areas and networks for creating evolutionarily novel abilities (e.g., reading, mathematics).

**Cognitive Systems and Innovation**

The evolutionary pressures that ramped up the human ability to adapt to novelty and change are described. These resulted in changes in the brain's top–down attentional control systems and the systems that support self-referential problem solving and integration of remotely related ideas (default mode network). These networks support general ability and creativity and can be engaged to modify primary folk systems to create new networks that support learning evolutionarily novel or biologically secondary abilities.

**Cumulative Cultural Evolution and Academic Learning**

The human ability to modify primary systems to create secondary abilities, along with social imitation and other factors, created a cumulative culture. Here, useful innovations are retained and transmitted to the next generation. This accumulated knowledge created the need for formal schooling to better prepare children for an adulthood that requires secondary knowledge and skills in these cultures.

**Foundations of Evolutionary Educational Psychology**

The foundational premises of evolutionary educational psychology are presented. The gist is that cumulative culture has created a gap between abilities that children easily acquire (e.g., language) through engagement in species-typical activities (e.g., social play) and the abilities they need to be successful in the modern world. The premises focus on the implications for instructional practices and students' academic motivation.

**Table 1** (cont.)

___

**Biologically Secondary Learning**

Evolutionary elaboration of the brain's top–down attentional control networks and plasticity in brain regions that support folk abilities opened the door for the creation and learning of evolutionarily novel abilities and skills, such as writing systems and mathematics. Cognitive and brain imaging studies are used to describe how instruction capitalizes on the language system to create the ability to read and write. The same approach is used to describe learning in biologically secondary mathematics.

**Noncognitive Processes and Educational Outcomes**

An evolutionary framework is used to integrate aspects of the attentional control and default mode networks with academic self-concepts, personality, and academic anxieties (e.g., math anxiety), and how these influence short-term and long-term educational outcomes.

**Conscientiousness and Anxiety**

One of attentional networks controls the switching between external and internal, self-referential attentional focus. The network is related to conscientiousness and the ability to maintain external focus during academic learning and to maintain long-term educational goals. A component of the network is also involved in acquired fears and likely contributes to academic anxieties.

**Self-Awareness and Academic Self-Concepts**

Evolutionary elaboration of the brain's default mode network supports self-awareness (focusing attention on and gaining knowledge about aspects of the self) and self-conceptions that in turn are the foundation for academic self-beliefs. These beliefs and awareness of academic strengths and weaknesses enable cultural niche seeking.

**Instruction Implications and Research**

The general educational implications of an evolutionary approach to academic learning are provided and focus on differences between the developmental activities that promote primary and secondary learning. These differences help to resolve long-standing debates about educational approaches.

___

variation in the relative enhancement of one conserved system or another. As an example, nocturnal primates have relatively larger olfactory than visual systems, whereas diurnal (awake during the day) species have relatively larger visual than olfactory systems (DeCasien & Higham, 2019).

In other words, species that are active at night are more dependent on smell to detect conspecifics (members of the same species), prey, and predators, whereas species that are active during the day are more dependent on visual cues for these same things. Evolutionary selection will favor individuals of nocturnal species with better olfactory than visual systems, and the opposite for individuals of diurnal species, resulting in differential enhancement of olfactory and visual systems. At the same time, there are unique aspects of brain structure and functions (e.g., patterns of gene expression) across orders (e.g., primates vs. rodents) and species (Bi et al., 2023; DeCasien et al., 2022). These differences can involve, for instance, the division of one brain area into subdivisions that process related but distinct types of information. Each of these areas might have related but more specialized functions (e.g., responding to different types of social cues) and with different patterns of connectivity to other brain areas. These differentiations could be unique to a particular species (e.g., humans vs. great apes) or unique to a group of related species (e.g., great apes vs. monkeys) (Preuss & Wise, 2022).

One important point is that evolution largely acts on integrated systems of brain regions that facilitate adaptive behaviors or cognitions, and many differences across species are in terms of the relative (controlling overall brain size) enhancement of the functioning of one system or another, and sometimes differentiation of some areas that can assume new functions. These coordinated brain regions tend to develop and fire synchronously, and their expression is influenced by overlapping genes (Alexander-Bloch et al., 2013; Arnatkeviciute et al., 2021). For instance, human language is supported by multiple interconnected brain areas. These areas codevelop and are influenced by a common set of genes, but these in turn differ from the system and underlying genes that influence stress and emotional reactivity (Thompson et al., 2001). Engagement in species-typical behaviors further ensures the synchronous activity of these brain networks and helps to solidify their integration during development and better adapt them to the nuances of local conditions.

The proposed evolved functions of these networks typically include some mix of coping with social demands, other species (e.g., avoiding predation), and the physical environment (e.g., navigating) (DeCasien et al., 2022; Sliwa & Freiwald, 2017). Associated debates concern the relative importance of one demand, such as dealing with conspecifics, or another, such as finding food that is dispersed across the ecology. The same is true for models of human cognitive evolution, with different proposals focused on the relative importance of coping with weather changes (e.g., preparing for winter) (Kanazawa, 2008; Potts, 1998), the need to become proficient in obtaining the staples of life (e.g., hunting) (Kaplan et al., 2000), and social dynamics (Alexander, 1989; Flinn et al., 2005; Geary, 2005). It is likely that some combination of these factors contributed to human cognitive evolution, but their relative importance may have changed over evolutionary time.

In any case, these pressures align with research on children's biologically primary or folk abilities, that is, an intuitive and universal understanding of people and social dynamics (folk psychology), other species (folk biology), and the physical world (folk physics). The key to the emergence of culture and the invention and eventual need to learn in academic or biologically secondary domains is an evolved ability to modify these folk abilities from the top down, that is, to reconfigure evolved brain networks so that they process and comprehend novel information. The ability to learn in these secondary domains has been studied for more than a century, and the underlying processes are called general ability or general intelligence (Spearman, 1904). The following sections overview primary domains, place general ability in an evolutionary perspective, and describe the evolutionary elaboration of the brain systems that support attentional control and self-referential thoughts and use of mental models for problem solving. These elaborations are components of humans' general ability and creativity and undergird human cultural evolution and contribute to the ability to modify primary systems during schooling.

## 2.1 Folk Domains

Primary abilities represent brain (e.g., Wernicke's area that supports language), perceptual (e.g., basic language sounds), and cognitive (e.g., language comprehension) systems that enable people to develop and manage social relationships, forage and hunt, construct tools, and remember and navigate in the local ecology. These abilities can be organized as folk psychology, folk biology, and folk physics (Atran, 1998; Geary, 2005; S. A. Gelman, 2003; Leslie et al., 2004; Mithen, 1996; Wellman & Gelman, 1992), as shown in Figure 1. The social level reflects competencies and knowledge that support social relationships and dynamics (Brothers & Ring, 1992; Dunbar, 1998; Flinn et al., 2005; Humphrey, 1976), whereas the ecological level (biological and physical) reflects competencies and knowledge that support survival activities, such as hunting or using plants as medicines, in traditional contexts (Kaplan et al., 2000). The third level is composed of key folk domains that can be put together in building-block form to create functional systems to meet current social or ecological demands (Geary, 2005). The Individual level under folk psychology, for example, captures the abilities (e.g., language, face processing) and knowledge (person schema) that are engaged during social interactions and that support social relationships.

These are not the final words on folk abilities, but nevertheless they provide an organization to the types of competencies that emerge and the ways in which knowledge is organized in the absence of schooling. The brain and cognitive systems that support primary abilities are also the raw materials from which secondary abilities are constructed and reflect the motivational and behavioral biases of children. These biases generate experiences (Section 2.1.3) that are needed for the full development of many primary abilities but at the same time might conflict with the motivation to engage in activities that promote secondary learning.

### 2.1.1 Folk Psychology

The folk psychological domains are organized around abilities and knowledge related to the self, individuals, and groups. These domains and those in the next section can be considered modular in that they represent integrated abilities and knowledge schemas (i.e., knowledge organized around a specific theme), but they are supported by systems of brain regions not a single region. Language, for instance, is a coherent and very functional social-cognitive ability but is supported by a system of regions that are distributed across various areas in the brain (Gernsbacher & Kaschak, 2003) and is highly integrated with other social competencies, such as use of gesture (Skipper et al., 2007).

*Self-awareness* is the ability to focus attention on attributes of the self and to mentally time travel, that is, to think about oneself in the past and to project oneself into potential future situations (Suddendorf & Corballis, 2007; Tulving, 2002). It is supported by the default mode (Section 2.2.3) and executive attention (Section 2.2.4) brain networks that act on personal (autobiographical) memories and other representations of the self (Lou et al., 2017; Raichle, 2015). One area of the default mode network is involved in feelings of agency, self-awareness, personal memories, and thinking about the world in self-relevant ways (Cavanna & Trimble, 2006; Rugg & Vilberg, 2013), whereas other areas support conscious reflections about the self, including self-evaluations (Davey et al., 2016). The combination allows people to generate a conscious representation of themselves in the context of past and future social scenarios (Andrews-Hanna et al., 2014) and to engage in social comparisons and to socially strategize (Geary, 2005; Raichle, 2015). The *self-schema* links autobiographical memories with knowledge and beliefs about the self. These beliefs include personal evaluations of competence in various areas (Bandura, 2001; Ryan & Deci, 2017), including academic self-concepts, self-efficacy, and in modern contexts anxiety around academics, including mathematics anxiety (Geary, 2022; Geary & Xu, 2022; Levine & Pantoja, 2021).

The *individual-level* competencies support the development and maintenance of one-on-one relationships and social interactions (Bugental, 2000; Caporael, 1997). These are supported by a suite of brain and cognitive systems that enable the ability to read nonverbal communication signals (e.g., gesture), facial expressions, language, and theory of mind (Adolphs, 1999; Brothers & Ring, 1992; Humphrey, 1976; Pinker & Bloom, 1990), and are integrated with social-reward, motivational, and emotional systems (Gangopadhyay et al., 2021). Theory of mind is the ability to make inferences about the intentions, beliefs, emotional states, and likely future behavior of other individuals and is especially developed in humans and related to social skills (Imuta et al., 2016; Leslie et al., 2004). People develop *person schemas* of familiar people and people for whom future relationships are expected (Fiske & Taylor, 1991). The schema is a long-term memory network that includes representations of other persons' physical attributes (e.g., sex, age), as well as memories for specific behavioral episodes, and more abstract trait information.

People typically live in large social groups and differentially affiliate with others. Behaviors and cognitions regarding these social groupings are influenced by kinship, the formation of ingroups and outgroups, and ideologically based social identification (Alexander, 1989; Dunbar, 1993). An evolved bias to favor kin over non-kin is found across species (W. D. Hamilton, 1964; Lukas & Clutton-Brock, 2018). The formation of ingroup coalitions composed of kin and oftentimes cooperating non-kin (e.g., friends) is common among primates and results in response to the formation of competing groups, that is, individuals in these groups cooperate to better compete with other groups (outgroups) over control of important resources (e.g., food sources).

The formation of ingroups and outgroups is a human universal, especially under threat. In these contexts, biases favoring ingroup members and hostile attributions (e.g., outgroup intends to harm the ingroup) about members of outgroups are exacerbated (Horowitz, 2001; Riek et al., 2006). Hewstone et al. (2002, p. 586) concluded that "threat is a central explanatory concept in several of the theories . . . and literature on intergroup bias." Humans have the unique ability to form large ingroups based on ideology and a shared system of beliefs and selectively applied moral rules (Abrams & Hogg, 1990). These are critical to the formation of larger and more competitive groups than would otherwise be possible based on personal relationships, and support collective action among ingroup members. Ultimately, alliances are about organizing groups that have common interests, and these interests are ultimately directed at gaining control of resources and status and the allocation of these to members of one's alliance (Geary, 2005; Pinsof et al., 2023).

## 2.1.2 Folk Biology and Folk Physics

Evolved adaptations that enable dealing with other species, specifically potential prey and predators, are the norm. For mammals and other complex organisms, there is ample evidence for species-specific brain, cognitive, behavioral, and physical specializations that enable the location and manipulation (e.g., raccoons, *Procyon lotor*, cleaning of food) of edible plants, fruits, and nuts, as well as the location and capture of prey species (e.g., Barton & Dean, 1993; Huffman et al.,1999). The *folk biology* systems shown in Figure 1 represent the most rudimentary cognitive specializations that support humans' ability to learn about, identify, and secure biological resources in natural contexts (Malt, 1995; Medin & Atran, 2004). As with folk psychological competencies, there appears to be an inherent but skeletal set of perceptual (e.g., attention to self-generated motion) and cognitive biases (e.g., inference that living things have agency) that orient children toward living things and support learning about them (Atran, 1998; Margett-Jordan et al., 2017; Setoh et al., 2013). By adolescence, these coalesce into functional competencies that support hunting, gathering, horticulture, and, in many contexts, animal domestication.

The result is that people throughout the world can categorize the flora and fauna in their local ecologies and show similar categorical and inferential biases when reasoning about them (Atran, 1998; Berlin et al., 1966). Through ethnobiological studies, "it has become apparent that, while individual societies may differ considerably in their conceptualization of plants and animals, there are a number of strikingly regular structural principles of folk biological classification which are quite general" (Berlin et al., 1973, p. 214). Knowledge of the species' morphology, behavior, growth pattern, and ecological niche help to define the essence of the species (Malt, 1995), which is a species-specific schema that includes knowledge of salient and stable characteristics (Medin et al., 2006). Biological essence allows people to mentally represent and predict the likely behavior of plants and animals, as related to hunting, foraging, and horticulture.

As shown in Figure 1, *folk physics* represents the brain, perceptual, and cognitive systems that support engagement with the physical world as related to seeking food, shelter, or mates and to avoid threats (e.g., predators) (Gallistel, 1990; O'Keefe, J., & Nadel, 1978). *Movement* captures the systems that support actual movement or navigation in physical space (Milner & Goodale, 2006). These are common, evolutionarily old systems that include the hippocampus, surrounding areas, and parts of the parietal and occipital cortices (Broglio et al., 2015; E. A. Murray et al., 2018). Exploration of the environment results in the development of implicit "cognitive maps" or representations of large-scale space that further aid in navigation. However, *representation* in Figure 1 refers to the ability to explicitly (from the top-down) generate and mentally manipulate maps or images of large-scale space and understand the orientation of objects to one another in this space even when not directly engaged in it.

*Tool use* refers to an understanding of the properties of objects, such as shape, and the ability to mentally represent images of objects in different positions. The latter contributes to an understanding of how objects can be used as tools and mechanical reasoning (Hegarty, 2004; Reynaud et al., 2016). The human ability to explicitly represent large-scale space, how objects move in space, and how they might be used as tools exceeds the capabilities of other species (e.g., Povinelli, 2000). The brain systems that support these various visuospatial abilities also include areas that enable the representation of relative magnitude, such as distance (Summerfield et al., 2020). These magnitudes are typically represented along a single continuous dimension that encodes the relations among them, such as closer to farther. The *number* system shown in Figure 1 is one of these dimensions – called the approximate number system (ANS) – and supports an intuitive understanding of relative quantity (Feigenson et al., 2004; Gallistel & Gelman, 2000; Geary et al., 2015). The ANS provides an intuitive sense of more versus less when comparing two or more groups of objects (e.g., potential food) and is mentioned here because of its potential relation to secondary mathematics.

### 2.1.3 Developmental Elaboration

The evolutionary enhancement of one brain area or system or another is realized during prenatal and postnatal development. For mammals and birds, this development can be influenced by intrinsic factors (e.g., patterns of inherent gene expression), termed the protomap hypothesis (Rakic, 1988), as well as by activity-dependent extrinsic factors (Greenough et al., 1987), termed the protocortex hypothesis (O'Leary et al., 1994). During human prenatal development, some areas of the brain (e.g., prefrontal cortex, visual cortex, below) show region-specific patterns of gene expression and specific genetic influences on the specialization of these areas, in keeping with the protomap hypothesis, whereas other regions appear to become specialized based in part on patterns of input from other brain regions, such as the thalamus (Bhaduri et al., 2021), in keeping with the protocortex hypothesis. Among other functions (e.g., contributions to cognitive and affective systems), the thalamus relays information from sensory and motor systems, such as sounds, to the cortex (Roy et al., 2022), and during prenatal development, it sends different patterns of signals to the neocortex that in turn contribute to the specialization of different brain

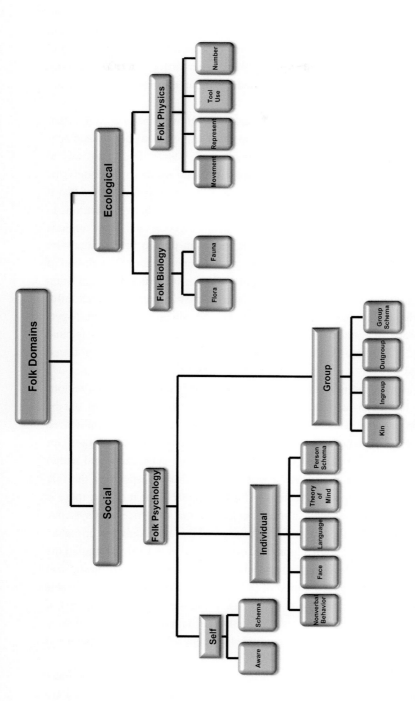

**Figure 1** Primary folk abilities coalesce around the domains of folk psychology, folk biology, and folk physics. These enable the navigation of core social relationships and the common ecological demands (e.g., hunting) of people living in traditional contexts. Adapted from *The origin of mind: Evolution of brain, cognition, and general intelligence*, by D. G. Geary, 2005, p. 129. Copyright 2005 by American Psychological Association.

regions for processing different types of information (e.g., sounds, visual images). The core point is that the basic structure of most mammalian brain regions emerges prenatally through patterns of region-specific processes, and many of these systems become refined and better differentiated by activity patterns (neural firing patterns) triggered by other regions (Cadwell et al., 2019).

For some species, extrinsic influences also arise from postnatal behaviors that result in species-typical or experience-expectant exposure to socially and ecologically important information (Greenough et al., 1987). This sensitivity to postnatal experiences is an important aspect of brain plasticity, although this form of plasticity is not yet fully understood. What is known indicates that it occurs at different levels (e.g., from synaptic connections between neurons to integrated brain systems) and can differ across species and brain regions (Bonfanti & Charvet, 2021). Plasticity is linked in part to brain maturation and thus slower-developing brains imply greater potential for the evolution of modifiable brain systems, which of course suggests important levels of brain plasticity in humans. At the same time, genetic constraint and hormonal influences during puberty are important influences on brain development that operate, in theory, in concert with experience-expectant activities (Arnatkeviciute et al., 2021; Bonfanti & Charvet, 2021), but how these interact is not well understood.

In any case, the point is that there are evolutionarily conserved brain regions whose basic structure and function emerge during prenatal development, but the maturation of some of these regions and systems of regions will be influenced by postnatal experiences. The benefit of such plasticity is likely largest for domains in which the associated demands vary across generations and within lifespans (Greenough et al., 1987), which includes many aspects of the folk domains shown in Figure 1 (Geary & Huffman, 2002). For instance, there is both constraint and plasticity in many social information processing systems. The basic structure of the human face is conserved (across people and primates) and there are dedicated brain regions that orient attention toward and support the processing of facial features, but aspects of the system are also plastic and function to support the recognition of individual people, such as one's parents (Johnson et al., 2015; Pascalis et al., 2002). There are also mixed patterns of regularity and variation in other folk psychological domains, and in folk biology and folk physics domains that allow people to occupy vastly different social and ecological niches.

Consider the auditory system (for processing sounds) as an example of constraint and plasticity. All mammals have basic auditory neocortical regions that form prenatally (Krubitzer, 1995; Northcutt & Kaas, 1995). Some regions of the human auditory system are specialized for processing speech sounds in infancy (Dehaene et al., 2010), and these become refined and more specialized based on postnatal exposure to language (Kuhl, 2010). The process of refining this brain system is aided by common patterns of parent–child synchronized vocalizations, parents' modified speech patterns (infant-directed speech), and infants' attention to such speech (Cox et al., 2023; Nguyen et al., 2022; Peter et al., 2016). These experience-expectant episodes aid in many aspects of infants' language development, including a trimming of the range of language sounds to which the system responds (Kuhl et al., 1997). One result is that the system becomes more sensitive to the parents' native language sounds and less sensitive to language sounds they have not heard.

A similar process, as noted, has been demonstrated for face processing (Johnson et al., 2015; Pascalis et al., 2002) and is likely critical for the development of many features of the folk domains shown in Figure 1 (Bjorklund, 2018; Geary & Bjorklund, 2000; Geary & Huffman, 2002). The basic idea is shown in Figure 2, whereby many of the early competencies of folk domains reflect innate but skeletal knowledge (R. Gelman, 1990; S. A. Gelman, 2003; Spelke et al., 1992). Skeletal means the underlying perceptual and cognitive systems that emerge during prenatal brain development provide the initial structure of folk competencies (e.g., orientation toward faces or natural speech patterns), and these are fleshed out and adapted to local conditions as children engage in species-typical or experience-expectant behaviors (R. Gelman, 1990; Gopnik & Wellman, 2012). For these processes to operate, early attentional, perceptual,

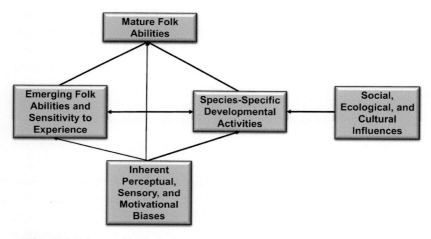

**Figure 2** Inherent biases influence infants' and children's emerging folk abilities and include biases in motivational and reward systems that promote child-initiated species-typical behaviors. These experiences result in neural activity patterns that refine and solidify folk abilities.

and cognitive biases must be coupled with a motivation to engage the ecology and the social world in ways that recapitulate the experiences that drove the evolution of these biases (Bjorklund & Pellegrini, 2002; Greenough, 1991; Scarr, 1992).

These behavioral biases are expressed as common childhood activities, including parent-child interactions, peer relationships, and exploration of the ecology, and are maintained because they likely trigger inherent reward centers (i.e., they are enjoyable). These activities result in experience-expectant activation of the brain systems that underlie folk domains. The result is a refinement of these skeletal systems such that they are better adapted to local conditions just as early exposure to language fine tunes the systems that process language sounds. To be sure, there are important and often substantive genetic influences on postnatal brain development, but there are also activity-dependent influences on aspects of this development (Jernigan et al., 2011; Thompson et al., 2001). The point is that some aspects of children's normal brain and cognitive development are dependent on co-evolving motivational and behavioral biases that result in the experiences needed for the full development and refinement of these brain and cognitive systems.

Based on evolutionary and prenatal and postnatal constraints on the structure and functioning of most of these brain regions, there are almost certainly constraints on how experience-expectant activities influence brain and cognitive development; that is, the brain though plastic is not a blank slate (Pinker, 2004). These built-in constraints are critically important from an educational perspective, because they indicate that the systems have evolved to process specific types of information within a constrained range and do not as readily (or ever) process information outside of this range (Geary & Huffman, 2002). These experience-expectant activities are contrasted with experience-dependent activities that are unique to the individual and result in individual-specific brain and cognitive representations of the environment (e.g., different people will have different schemas for their close friends).

## 2.2 Cognitive Systems and Innovation

Although the systems that support folk domains only process a specific range of information (e.g., language sounds, object features), the plasticity of these systems means some of them can be modified to process evolutionarily novel information that does not differ too much from the evolved counterpart. The core levels of plasticity include the potential to modify specific brain regions to process novel information (e.g., increase in synaptic connections or changes in these connections), such as letters and numerals, and to create novel integrated systems of brain regions that support more complex academic competencies. Indeed, the foundation of human innovation, including scientific, technical, and artistic advances, is the ability to modify evolved folk domains and create a deeper conceptual understanding of the social, biological, and physical worlds (Geary, 2007).

An example is provided by a contrast of naïve (folk physics) beliefs about the forces acting on a thrown object and Newton's (1687/1995) analysis of objects in motion in his masterwork, *The Principia*. Adults and children can typically (not always) describe the correct trajectory of a thrown or moving object (e.g., Kaiser et al., 1986), reflecting their implicit folk competencies. However, most people believe there is a force propelling a thrown object forward and a force propelling it downward. The downward force is gravity (later revised by Einstein), but there is no force propelling it forward, once the object leaves the individual's hand (Clement, 1982). The concept of a forward-force is like pre-Newtonian beliefs about motion prominent among natural philosophers in the fourteenth to sixteenth centuries. Newton's conceptual depiction of object motion (first law of motion in this case) advanced this naïve folk concept, and he said as much: "I do not define time, space, place and motion, as being well known to all. Only I must observe, that the vulgar conceive those quantities under no other notions but from the relation they bear to sensible objects" (Newton, 1687/1995, p. 13). These were later reinterpreted by Einstein to provide an even more accurate understanding of motion, time, and space.

Newton's core stepping stone for modern physics might seem ancient, given it was published in 1687, but this is just the blink of an eye relative to the 200,000-year history of modern humans, and of course Einstein's contributions in the early twentieth century were even more recent. The point is that scientific and many other cultural advances (e.g., Haydn's refinement of the structure of classical symphonies) are very recent from an evolutionary perspective, and, unlike folk abilities, their emergence is not universal (C. Murray, 2003). The critical point is that there has not been sufficient time or sufficient evolutionary advantages to create dedicated brain systems and motivational and behavioral biases to easily acquire these new forms of knowledge. It is not a coincidence that formal schooling, and eventually universal schooling, emerged in times and places in which evolutionarily novel innovations were emerging (Geary, 2002, 2007).

At the same time, humans are clearly capable of creating and learning these forms of evolutionarily novel knowledge. One goal of the evolutionary approach to education is to determine the best ways it can capitalize on this plasticity to coax the brain to process information and grasp concepts that do not have the same types of built-in scaffolds that support folk abilities. The sections below provide a theoretical framework for conceptualizing the evolutionary pressures that resulted in the ability to create and learn novel knowledge, and a later section addresses educational implications.

### 2.2.1 Evolution of General Ability

A key benefit of brain plasticity is the ability to adapt to novelty and change, but there are cost-benefit trade-offs common to biological systems (Williams, 1957), and thus high levels of plasticity are not expected to be a feature of all brain areas. The most basic trade-offs are illustrated in Figure 3 and can only be appreciated in the context of the ecologies in which the species' evolved (Dukas, 1998). From this perspective, brain, perceptual, and cognitive systems provide the interface between the organism and the ecology and function to guide the organisms' behavior to achieve outcomes that enhance survival or

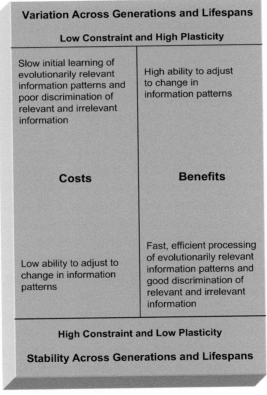

**Figure 3** The rectangle highlights cost-benefit trade-offs that are predicted to influence the evolution of brain and cognitive plasticity. Adapted from "Brain and cognitive evolution: Forms of modularity and functions of mind," by D. C. Geary and K. J. Huffman, 2002, *Psychological Bulletin, 128*, p. 668. Copyright 2002 by the American Psychological Association. Reprinted with permission.

reproductive prospects in these ecologies. Selection will favor brain and cognitive systems that are modifiable through activity-dependent changes to the extent survival- and reproduction-related information varies across generations and within life spans. The result is the ability to modify (within limits) these systems to better fit local conditions. Selection will favor inherent constraints to the extent these information patterns are stable across generations and within life spans, which ensures the fast and accurate processing of this information. From this perspective, different brain and cognitive systems are predicted to vary with respect to relative degree of openness and constraint to the extent the associated information patterns are variable or stable, respectively.

Without inherent constraint, perception and cognition would be vulnerable to random, fleeting early experiences that could push brain development in ways that are not functional in the long term, whereas ubiquitous constraint would result in highly specialized and efficient perceptual and cognitive systems but with no potential to innovate if conditions change. A full understanding of brain and cognitive plasticity and the ability to create and learn (and better teach) novel things requires an understanding of the conditions that favored the ability to adapt to variation and change.

There are several proposals about humans' evolved ability to adapt to change, at least at the level of complex cognitive abilities. The proposals focus on the benefits of foresight, planning, and learning to anticipate and prepare for variation in seasonal changes (e.g., winter, monsoon season) (Kanazawa, 2008; Potts, 1998), to become proficient in obtaining the staples of life (e.g., hunting) (Kaplan et al., 2000), or to compete with other people or groups of people for control of social dynamics and critical resources (Alexander, 1989; Flinn et al., 2005; Geary, 2005). All these conditions create dynamic change and selection would favor those with the ability to adapt to this change, although there are other ways to adapt (e.g., migrating when the weather changes), and thus any such adaptations need not be found across all species. It is likely that some combination of these factors contributed to the evolution of complex cognitive abilities that support adaptation to novelty, although their relative importance may have changed across evolutionary time (Bailey & Geary, 2009).

Ecological changes in Africa during hominin (our direct ancestors) evolution are well documented and would have resulted in changing weather patterns and changing food sources, which has been proposed as a driver of brain evolution (Vrba, 1996). One difficulty with this climate-ecology argument is that sympatric (living in same ecology) primate species did not experience the same change in brain size as our direct ancestors (Elton et al., 2001) and their decedents do not show the same ability to adapt to novelty as modern humans. Social competition explains the apparent contradiction because it could result in a within-species arms race that would separate our relatively more recent ancestors' brain and cognitive evolution from that of other species living in the same ecology (Alexander, 1989; Flinn et al., 2005). The basic idea is that *Homo erectus* and later *Homo sapiens* expanded into new ecologies and became increasingly skilled at exploiting them. These gains in ecological dominance resulted in the crossing of an evolutionary Rubicon:

> the ecological dominance of evolving humans diminished the effects
> of "extrinsic" forces of natural selection such that within-species
> competition became the principle "hostile force of nature" guiding
> the long-term evolution of behavioral capacities, traits, and tendencies.
> (Alexander, 1989, p. 458)

Humans' emerging ecological dominance is consistent with the increased rate of megafauna extinction following human migration into their ranges (P. S. Martin, 1973). More generally, when a species migrates into an unexploited region with abundant resources, as our ancestors did, the result is relatively low levels of social competition and rapid increases in population size, as shown by the top oval in Figure 4 (Mac Arthur & Wilson, 1967). As the population expands, the per capita resources necessarily decline and competition for access to them necessarily intensifies, as was described by Malthus (1798) for many human populations in developing nations before the demographic shift and M. J. Hamilton and Walker (2018) for hunter-gatherer societies. The increase in social competition is represented by the rightmost oval of Figure 4. Under these conditions, Darwin and Wallace's (1858, p. 54) conceptualization of natural selection as a "struggle for existence" becomes in addition a struggle with other people for control of the resources that support life and allow one to reproduce (Geary, 2005). The eventual result is a population crash, after which the per capita availability of resources is higher than it was before the crash. A well-documented example is the increase in laborers' wages and standard of living following plague-induced population crashes in the mid fourteenth century (Clark, 2016). Following such crashes, another cycle of population expansion to the carrying capacity of the ecology and later contraction begins (Fanta et al., 2018).

The repeating cycle accelerates evolutionary selection and will favor those individuals who gain enhanced social influence and control over culturally important resources (Geary, 2021; Winegard et al., 2018a). There are many ways to achieve advantage, and at least some of these are likely facilitated by general ability and creative innovation. As shown in Figure 4, my proposal is that general ability and creativity facilitated the creation of novel

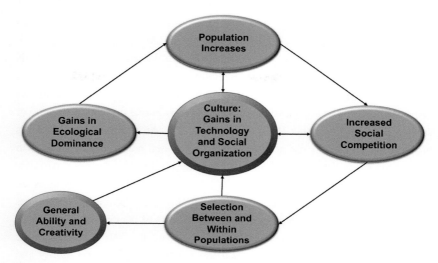

**Figure 4** A cyclical within-species arms race likely contributed to evolutionary changes in social and technological complexity and supporting changes in brain and cognition. Adapted from "Mitochondrial functions, cognition, and the evolution of intelligence: Reply to commentaries and moving forward." By D. C. Geary, 2020 *Journal of Intelligence*, *8*, p. 14. Copyright 2020 by author.

technologies, social strategies, and patterns of social organization that not only resulted in competitive advantage but further gains in these areas. We cannot of course directly study the associated social dynamics among earlier species of *Homo* or early modern humans, but the historical record supports the proposal.

The emergence of large-scale agricultural societies illustrates the dynamics. Although diet quality was often lower than that of hunters and gatherers, agriculture increased available calories and supported population growth, which in turn resulted in competitive advantages over smaller groups (Clark, 2008). These additional calories were often stored as grain reserves or in livestock and created a source of wealth that could be, and was, raided (Hirschfeld, 2015; Turchin, 2009). Large-scale conflicts often emerged in areas in which steppes occupied by nomadic herders abutted fertile agricultural lands (Turchin, 2009). In these contexts, many nomadic groups began raiding agricultural settlements. The latter prompted the defensive formation of larger agricultural communities, which was then countered by the unification of disparate nomadic groups. This cyclical pattern appears to have emerged in many parts of the world and was associated with advances in social

organization, military strategy, and technology, and eventually led to the formation of empires (Currie et al., 2020; Hermann et al., 2020; Turchin et al., 2013).

These cultural advances must have been aided, at least in part, by individuals
with traits that fostered innovation, including strong general problem-solving
abilities, foresight, and creativity, such as skill at synthesizing information across
disparate domains or the use of analogical relations in one domain to reframe or
solve a problem in another (De Dreu et al., 2023). An example of the latter is
provided by Torricelli's use of the weight of water and pressure felt by divers to
understand the weight of air or air pressure and to refine the design of mercury
barometers to measure it (Middleton, 1963). Innovation and cultural advances are
likely facilitated by other traits, such as rationality (i.e., the ability to suppress
cognitive biases while problem solving), and aspects of personality (Schmidt &
Hunter, 2004; Stanek & Ones, 2023; Stanovich et al., 2016). Whatever the
combination of traits, one result is that the importance of general ability and
abilities underlying innovation would increase with increases in the complexity of
social groups, technologies, and other cultural innovations (e.g., monetary systems). General ability (Section 2.2.2) would be broadly important because success in these cultural contexts would have been increasingly dependent on ease of
learning the novel advances made by others. Thus, it is not surprising that formal
education independently arose in these types of early large-scale societies (e.g.,
Mesopotamia, ancient Egypt) and involved the training of scribes in literacy and
numeracy to help with the bureaucratic management of these societies (Eskelson,
2020). Note that the inclusion of general ability and creativity in this model
focuses only on their effects on enhancing social influence and access to survival-
and reproduction-related resources, which sometimes resulted in advances (e.g.,
weaponry) that might be considered prosocial and widely beneficial and at other
times destructive (Sternberg, 2021).

### 2.2.2 Integrating Psychometric and Evolutionary Models

The evolutionary approach to brain and cognition needs to be reconciled with
more than a century of psychometric research on human cognitive abilities
(Geary, 2005). The latter focuses on individual differences in performance on
various types of perceptual, cognitive, and academic tests. As shown in
Figure 5, performance on these tests has revealed that human abilities are
hierarchically organized, with specific skills and knowledge (not shown) at
the lowest level (e.g., arithmetic, algebra), broader abilities (e.g., visuospatial,
mathematics) at the next level, and general ability at the apex (Carroll, 1993;
McGrew, 2009). This means that performance on tests at lower levels is influenced by knowledge or abilities at the next level. So, people with generally

**Figure 5** Psychometric research indicates that cognitive abilities are hierarchically organized. At the lowest strata (not shown) are narrow domains of knowledge (e.g., arithmetic, algebra, geometry) that have a core cognitive process or knowledge base in common and are represented by a higher strata ability (e.g., Math Abilities). Performance in all domains is influenced by general ability.

strong mathematics knowledge do better than others in specific areas of mathematics. General ability influences performance on all tests regardless of their content.

These hierarchies provide useful information on the organization of human knowledge and abilities, at least for people living in modern contexts, but differ from the folk domains shown in Figure 1. Some aspects overlap, as in the consistent identification of visuospatial (aspects of folk physics) and auditory/verbal (aspects of folk psychology) abilities in folk domains and psychometric studies, but there are also clear differences (e.g., Thurstone & Thurstone, 1941). The structure of these hierarchies depends on the measures used in the studies, and most of these include measures of evolutionarily novel abilities, such as mathematics, and reading measures, and not measures of folk abilities, such as sensitivity to variation in facial expressions or theory of mind. As a result, the full diversity of individual differences in human cognition has yet to be determined.

In any case, the focus here is on what is known about general ability, that is, the brain and cognitive processes that are common to all forms of perception and cognition (Spearman, 1904). General ability (or general intelligence, g) likely results from a combination of factors at different levels, including cellular energy production (Geary, 2018), neuron development and intercellular synaptic functions (Gong et al., 2019; Sniekers et al., 2017), large-scale brain networks (Jung & Haier, 2007; Santarnecchi et al., 2017), and cognitive processes. Much of the research on the latter has focused on people's ability to identify the underlying rules or concepts in novel problem-solving domains (e.g., matrix reasoning), that is, fluid intelligence. These abilities in turn are thought to be supported by some combination of speed of information process- ing (Jensen & Munro, 1979), working memory (the ability to keep information in mind while engaged in other processes) (Engle et al., 1999), and top–down attentional control (Burgoyne & Engle, 2020; Kane & Engle, 2002).

In other words, the core functional competence, fluid intelligence, is the ability to problem solve, learn, and adapt to novel situations (Cattell, 1963; Horn & Cattell, 1966), and these in turn are supported by more basic abilities, such as top–down attentional control, which in turn are undergirded by under- lying neurobiological systems. The psychometric focus on the ability to prob- lem solve in novel contexts is consistent with the focus on variation and novelty in the evolutionary models. However, this does not tell us how problem solving unfolds and how it contributes to evolutionarily novel learning.

Recall that aspects of brain development occur based on activity-dependent external inputs; that is, the organization and functioning of many brain areas are enhanced when they are activated (e.g., synchronized cell firing) by inputs from other brain areas or based on experiences in the external world. Activation of one brain system or another is enhanced by attentional focus on the associated infor- mation (Cowan, 1998). Built-in perceptual systems (e.g., to orient toward faces) and motivational biases (e.g., to socially interact) ensure the repeated attention to and activation of the brain systems that support folk domains. This feature of the brain is critical to evolutionarily novel learning, but in these cases top–down attentional control is the key. Stated differently, learning evolutionarily novel skills or concepts will require repeated activation of the supporting brain systems as with folk abilities, but now top–down attentional control and internal and external organization of the materials to be learned are necessary to coax the brain into processing information (e.g., as in reading words) and grasping concepts (e.g., air pressure) that it is not fully pre-prepared to learn.

As with folk domains, activity-dependent modification of brain regions to process evolutionarily novel information can occur through use of internally generated mental models (e.g., understanding the behavior of a fictional character) or through external focus on novel information (e.g., passages in a book). The brain's default mode network is important for the generation of mental models and is likely critical to the self-generated internal representa- tion of novel information and concepts, whereas the executive attention or fronto-parietal network is important for overriding folk biases and maintain- ing attentional focus on to-be-learned novel external information. These are two of the core networks within the human brain (Yeo et al., 2011) and are related to the generation of creative or innovative ideas (default mode net- work) and the explicit evaluation of the feasibility or utility of these ideas (executive attention) (Marron et al., 2018; Simonton, 2003). The latter is also a core system that contributes to general ability, including competence at using step-by-step testing and evaluation of potential novel solutions to problems, as well as ease of learning in school (Jung & Haier, 2007; Kriegbaum et al., 2018). In other words, the within-species arms race resulted in elaboration of several core brain networks, including those associated with general ability and creative innovation.

### 2.2.3 Mental Models and the Default Mode Network

Building on the work of Alexander (1989), Humphrey (1976), and others (e.g., Johnson-Laird), Geary (2005) proposed that one component of general ability is competence at generating top–down self-centered mental models of current and potential future states and to use problem solving to generate and mentally rehearse strategies that could reduce the difference between these states. The earlier mentioned default mode network (DMN) contributes to this ability and to mentally problem solve, often focused on social problems and social strategizing (Udochi et al., 2022; Yeshurun et al., 2021), as do the executive attention networks (next section).

Critically, consistent with a within-species arms race, there is evidence for evolutionary elaboration of this network in humans. Relative to chimpanzees (*Pan troglodytes*) and macaque monkeys (genus *Macaca*) the DMN is disproportionately larger in humans than expected based on overall brain size, and genes that show signatures of relatively recent evolutionary selection are disproportionately expressed in the areas that compose this network, such as Brodmann areas 9, 10, and 24 in Figure 6 (Buckner & DiNicola, 2019; Wei et al., 2019). There is also evidence for increased integration of the DMN across primate evolution, with humans showing more integration of areas that enable the top–down generation of mental models than other primates (Garin et al., 2022), and likely better integration of current external activities (e.g., a conversation) with self-relevant beliefs (Yeshurun et al., 2021). In fact, the architecture of this network in evolutionarily distant relatives (e.g., lemurs, *Lemuroidea*) does not include mechanisms that would support the top–down generation of a human-like mental model (i.e., it is unlikely they can imagine social scenarios). The chimpanzee DMN is more similar to that of humans, including engagement of parts of the system when watching social interactions (Barks et al., 2015), but the extent to which they can engage these systems to imagine future social scenarios is not fully understood (Martin-Ordas, 2020).

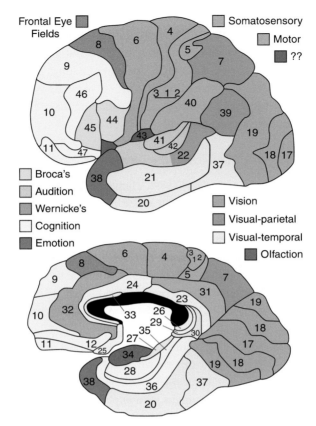

**Figure 6** Maps of Brodmann's (1909) areas of the human neocortex. The top section is the lateral (outer) view of the cortex, whereas the bottom section is the medial (center) view. Broca's and Wernicke's areas are part of the language system. Illustration courtesy of Mark Dubin.

For people, the network is most active during relaxed states and results in reflections that provide "a self-centered predictive model of the world" (Raichle, 2015, p. 443). The precuneus (area 7, Figure 6) is an important component of the network and contributes to the earlier noted feelings of agency, self-awareness, personal (episodic) memories, and thinking about the world in ways that involve the self (Cavanna & Trimble, 2006; Rugg & Vilberg, 2013), and the medial prefrontal area (e.g., areas 47 and 25 in Figure 6) contributes to conscious top–down reflections about the self, including explicit goal-directed self-evaluations, retrieval of episodic memories, and thinking about other people (Davey et al., 2016; Konu et al., 2020; Mancuso et al., 2022; Smallwood et al., 2021). The content of these thoughts supports the proposal that social pressures were significant contributors to human brain and cognitive evolution:

> The content of self-generated thoughts suggests that they serve an adaptive purpose by allowing individuals to prepare for upcoming events, form a sense of self-identity and continuity across time, and navigate the social world. On average, adults tend to rate their thoughts as goal oriented and personally significant, yet thoughts also commonly involve other people. (Andrews-Hanna et al., 2014, p. 32)

These thoughts often involve mental simulations of past, present, or potential future states (called prospective memory) that can be cast in language or as episodic memories (Rugg & Vilberg, 2013; Suddendorf & Corballis, 2007; Tulving, 2002). The integration of mental time travel and mental models for problem solving (Johnson-Laird, 1983) results in a uniquely human ability to construct self-centered representations of past, present, and potential future worlds and to engage in effortful reasoning and problem solving on the content of these representations. The future that people think about often involves a representation of a desired or fantasized state that can be compared to one's current situation. People typically have enhanced social status and more resources in this imagined future state relative to their current one. This future state is thus a goal to be achieved, and explicit social strategizing and problem solving enable people to plan ways to reduce the difference between where they are today and where they want to be in the future (Geary, 2005). The advantages that result from the ability to mentally simulate and rehearse various alternative future situations likely contributed to the evolutionary enhancement of the DMN. Stated differently, the DMN is likely a key component of the General Ability and Creativity component of the dynamics represented by Figure 4.

The default mode network is not simply about social problem solving, as subareas are activated when current tasks require integrating previously learned knowledge with current demands to aid in here-and-now decision making (Smallwood et al., 2021). More generally, the DMN integrates information across basic sensory and perceptual systems and forms representations about more abstract features of the world. Experiences with individual friends help to flesh out the person schema component of folk psychology for each of them, whereas commonalities across relationships and social interactions lead to more abstract people knowledge. For instance, people vary across two abstract dimensions of social behavior and focus, termed "agentic" and "communal." The former "revolves around independence, goal pursuit, and achievement, and the other revolves around other-focus, social orientation, and desire for connection" (A. E. Martin & Slepian, 2021, p. 1143). Girls and women have more communal traits, whereas boys and men have more agentic ones (Eagly, 1987). These differences in communal and agentic behaviors are abstracted and accurate stereotypes that reflect average sex differences in these areas, although any individual can deviate from the sex-typical average (Geary, 2021).

The DMN also forms abstract representations of common features of the physical word, such as its three-dimensional structure, and presumably the biological world, although these may engage additional areas of the parietal cortex and the executive attention networks (Section 2.2.4). The ability to form these abstract representations, generate mental models of the world, and to manipulate these representations to evaluate the potential outcomes of one action or another are likely core aspects of the ability to innovate and discover in science, technology, and the arts (Geary, 2007; Gotlieb et al., 2019). As mentioned, the DMN has been implicated in creative cognition, such as making associations between seemingly remote phenomena, and is often experienced as mind wandering (Andrews-Hanna et al., 2017; Konu et al., 2020; Kühn et al., 2014; Marron et al., 2018). The contribution to innovation appears to result, in part, from the dynamic interaction between two subsystems of the DMN: one that generates images, word associations, and mental time travel (more posterior areas), and one that involves a top–down control and evaluation of the flow of these thoughts (more anterior areas). This is experienced as internally focused attention with a mildly constrained train of images and thoughts focused on a particular end goal. In this case, the goal is to solve a novel problem. This can be seen in the descriptions of the problem-solving approaches of some innovators. In response to a query by Hadamard (1945) as to how he approached scientific questions, Einstein replied:

> The words of the language as they are written or spoken,
> do not seem to play any role in my mechanism of thought.
> The psychical entities which seem to serve as elements in
> thought are certain signs and more or less clear images which
> can be "voluntarily" reproduced and combined. . . . There is, of
> course, a certain connection between those elements and relevant
> logical concepts.
>
> *(Hadamard, 1945, p. 142)*

Hadamard (1945, p. 143) also noted that Einstein "refers to a narrowness of consciousness," which appears to have referred to sustained attention and the inhibition of distracting information while working on scientific questions, which likely involved the executive attention system. Einstein's accomplishments are, of course, unusual, but his descriptions of how he achieved some of his insights are of interest. This is because they are consistent with an attention-driven use of mental simulations that involve a top–down engagement of some of the basic visuospatial abilities that compose folk physics. Stated differently, it appears that Einstein intentionally engaged the DMN to form mental simulations that used folk physics representations (e.g., moving images) as part of his problem solving. The intuitive results from these simulations required mathematical proof that would have engaged executive attention, including the fronto-parietal network.

### 2.2.4 Deliberate Thought and the Executive Attention Networks

Orienting to the external world and selectively attending to potential threats or opportunities is critical to survival and reproduction. Such orienting is sometimes driven by automatic, bottom–up processing of certain types of stimuli, such as the biological motion of a prey species (Barton & Dean, 1993), but at other times, attention can be focused from the top–down, even with potentially distracting internal or external information. Attentional focus on important external (or internally generated) information results from the dynamic interactions among several brain networks (Menon & D'Esposito, 2022), including the salience, fronto-parietal, and cingulo-opercular network. The salience network focuses attention on specific goal-relevant information and contributes to the coordination of multiple other networks to respond to this information (Uddin, 2015). The network includes the anterior cingulate cortex (areas 24, 32, 33 in Figure 6) and insula (not shown in Figure 6), which in combination focus attention on changes in well-being (e.g., pain). In contrast, the cingulo-opercular network (including parts of area 24, Figure 6) is engaged when a sustained level of alertness is needed to achieve the goal (Coste & Kleinschmidt, 2016). The fronto-parietal network (including areas 9, 40, and 46, Figure 6) is important for the attentional control needed for step-by-step problem solving (Barbey, 2018). These networks have core hubs in the prefrontal cortex and their combination supports a top–down control of attention and problem solving, which at a functional level is often called executive attention (Witt et al., 2021; Yeo et al., 2011).

The executive attention networks operate in concert with other networks (depending on the task) and broadly support executive functions. The latter is composed of working memory or updating (the ability to hold information in mind while simultaneously performing another task), shifting (the ability to shift attention from one task to another and back), as well as general attentional control that influences the efficiency of engaging in updating and shifting and inhibiting distracting information (Miyake & Friedman, 2012). Comparisons of humans and other primates across behavioral studies of attentional performance and underlying brain systems indicate significant evolutionary change in the executive attention networks during human evolution. Behavioral studies of various primate species indicate enhanced attentional competencies, such as the ability to maintain attention in the face of distractors, but these are at about the level found in young children (less than seven years) and considerably lower than that of human adults (Beran et al., 2016; Posner, 2023).

At a neural level, engagement of executive attention typically involves the dynamic interaction between individual networks (e.g., salience, fronto-parietal), and often includes integration of activity across the anterior cingulate cortex, areas in the dorsolateral prefrontal cortex and areas in the parietal cortex, among others. The core of this network appears to be evolutionarily old, but is more differentiated in primates than in other mammals and more differentiated in humans than in other primates (Preuss & Wise, 2022). Moreover, many of the brain areas that support the executive attention networks are disproportionately larger in humans than would be expected based on the overall brain size (Wei et al., 2019). There also appears to have been evolutionary modifications of the white matter connectivity between these prefrontal regions and the attentional regions in the parietal cortex (Hecht et al., 2015). Although much remains to be learned, the combination of behavioral and brain imaging studies is in keeping with an evolutionary enhancement of humans' ability to engage in nuanced top–down attentional control in the service of complex, multistep problem solving.

As an example of these potential evolutionary changes, two components of the salience network, the anterior cingulate cortex and insula (involved in processing emotional and physical states, not shown in Figure 6), have a more integrated neural architecture in humans than in other primates and contribute to attention switching and attentional control (Molnar-Szakacs & Uddin, 2022; Posner et al., 2009; Uddin, 2015). The anterior cingulate is activated when goal achievement requires dealing with some degree of novelty, or conflict (e.g., choosing between two alternatives), in social or nonsocial contexts (Burgos-Robles et al., 2019; Monosov et al., 2020). For instance, in foraging primates, activity in the anterior cingulate, insula, and integrated areas influence whether they stay in the current location or move to a potentially more rewarding one. Activity in the anterior cingulate tracks the reward value (e.g., available food) of the current location and the reward value of alternative previously visited locations. When cingulate activity associated with memory of the latter exceeds the value of the current location, the animal switches. In a sense, cingulate activity and activity in the broader network signals the potential near-future gains of moving to a new location. In these situations, memories support a primitive form of mental time travel, but the anticipated future state is based on an amalgam of related past experiences. The trigger to switch appears to be automatic and the travel to the new foraging site is based solely on memories.

For people, the anterior cingulate and the wider salience network are also engaged in choice or conflict situations and can result in an attentional shift to the associated information and activation of the fronto-parietal network (Botvinick et al., 2001). A key difference is that the triggering of the latter enables more sustained attentional focus relative to other primates and supports prolonged engagement in explicit step-by-step problem solving that is focused on coping with the novel situation or resolving the conflict. With sufficient practice, these new and complex problem-solving approaches are committed to long-term memory and can be reused (automatically, with enough practice) in similar contexts. The difference between near-future states that are simply represented as a composite of memories and the ability to explicitly generate alternatives that never happened but potentially could is one key to human learning and part of the General Ability and Creativity component of Figure 4 (Geary, 2005).

Typically, engagement of the executive attention networks, especially the fronto-parietal network, results in deactivation of the default mode network, but their combination is often required to generate novel or creative solutions to current or anticipated future problems (Gotlieb et al., 2019). The default mode network contributes to imagining various alternative solutions to problems, especially social ones, and connecting disparate ideas, while the fronto-parietal network contributes to the implementation and evaluation of potential solutions. The process involves flexible switching – through the salience network – between the default mode and fronto-parietal networks (Andrews-Hanna et al., 2014; Heinonen et al., 2016), with this combination being particularly important for the evaluation of internally generated information (Beaty et al., 2015). The latter might involve mentally simulating an argument to influence the behavior of a friend. A mental model of this type affords the opportunity to explore the potential consequences of one argument or another and to generate responses to potential counterarguments.

Again, the divergence in the ability of humans and other primates, including our closest relatives, to engage in these prolonged attention-dependent mental simulations and problem solving is consistent with a within-species arms race. Circling back to the Developmental Elaborations section (Section 2.1.3), recall that many aspects of brain development are dependent on activation of the brain area or co-activation of networked areas. These are typically studied in the context of actual experiences that occur through triggers from other brain regions or from engagement in species-typical experience-expectant activities, such as social play (Greenough et al., 1991). Enhanced attentional control enables the inhibition of experience-expectant activities and attentional biases and engagement in activities that are not species typical, and a corresponding activation of brain areas or networks that would not typically occur. Moreover, the use of mental models allows people to generate at least some level of activity in these brain areas or networks in the absence of direct engagement with the environment.

In summary, the gist is that the General Ability and Creativity component of Figure 4 resulted from a within-species arms race that in turn resulted in human-specific enhancements of the default mode network and the executive-attention networks. The combination supports the top–down formation of mental models that can be used to generate and explicitly evaluate potential solutions to changing dynamics or to solve novel problems. The use of mental models allows people to think about things that have not happened and generate all sorts of various potential outcomes and solutions to novel problems. Top–down control of these models enables an explicit evaluation of the feasibility of one strategy or another and likely results in the activation of brain areas or co-activation of areas in ways that would not happen through engagement in species-typical behaviors. My argument is that the latter combined with inherent plasticity in some brain areas and networks support the ability to create and learn biologically secondary knowledge.

## 3 Cumulative Cultural Evolution and Academic Learning

Folk domains (Figure 1) represent universal forms of cognition because they reflect common evolutionary pressures (Geary, 2005), that is, coping with the competing interests of other people (folk psychology), securing food and avoiding predation (folk biology), and navigating within and sometimes changing (e.g., using tools) the ecology (folk physics). As was described in Section 2.1.3, the full development of many of the associated brain, perceptual, and cognitive systems is dependent on children's engagement in species-typical experience-expectant activities that result in activation of these systems and adapts them to local conditions. The importance of engaging in these experience-expectant activities would favor the evolution of associated motivational and reward systems that keep people focused on these domains. This focus along with the unrelenting importance of dealing with the social, biological, and physical worlds should organize cultural change and technical advances around these same themes; academic disciplines, for instance, fall into these three categories, with humanities and the social sciences related to folk psychology; biology, zoology, and forestry related to folk biology; and much of mathematics as well as physics and engineering related to folk physics.

Anthropologists and primatologists refer to these advances and their cross-generational transmission as cumulative cultural evolution (e.g., Dean et al., 2014; Richerson & Boyd, 2005). From this perspective, culture includes knowledge (e.g., ancestor tales, technologies), routines, and social rules that are useful to the group and are at least partially socially transmitted within and across generations. Cultural evolution occurs when knowledge or technologies are modified in ways that make them more useful than the original, and these advances are then transmitted to the next generation. Social transmission of useful knowledge, such as foraging routes or use of basic tools, has been documented in some nonhuman species (Whiten & Van Schaik, 2007), but whether these are modified to make them more useful and then transmitted (e.g., through imitation) across generations is debated (Dean et al., 2014; Mesoudi & Thornton, 2018).

Human cumulative cultural evolution in contrast is not debated (Tomasello, 1999). Lehman (1946) documented rapid and exponentially increasing gains in cultural knowledge over the past millennia in various scientific disciplines, mathematics, economics, philosophy, music, and other areas. The general trend was that the number of gains (e.g., scientific discoveries) for each twenty-five-year epoch was larger than the gains of the preceding epoch and that most of the knowledge in these areas emerged only in past few centuries (C. Murray, 2003). Many of these cultural changes can be seen as a continuation of eco-logical dominance, that is, the development of technologies (e.g., housing, refrigeration of food) and refinements in social organization (e.g., insurance to distribute risk) that reduce the risks in life. Derex (2022) proposed that these changes encompass both refinement and optimization of existing knowledge and technologies (e.g., using heat to harden spear tips) and the innovative development of qualitatively better ones through unique combinations, such as adding peddles and gears to draisines (Figure 7) to create early bikes.

The cognitive mechanisms that contribute to these abilities are debated and not yet fully understood (Dean et al., 2014), but they can be respectively integrated with what is known about the executive attention networks (fronto-parietal, salience) and the default mode network and with two common routes to creative contributions, that is, step-by-step incremental improvement and innovation through novel combinations of ideas (De Dreu et al., 2023; C. Murray, 2003; Simonton, 2003). In this view, the discontinuity between human cumulative cultural evolution and that of other species is due to the within-species arms race that resulted in the evolutionary modification of the executive attention and default mode networks (among others) during homi-nin evolution. Social competition ensures continued benefits to optimization and innovation and an unrelenting accumulation of new knowledge and technologies (Winegard et al., 2018a).

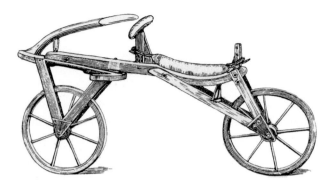

**Figure 7** Early nineteenth-century draisine. Creative Commons License. https://commons.wikimedia.org/wiki/File:DraisineI.jpg. In the Public Doman.

### 3.1 Foundations of Evolutionary Educational Psychology

The rapid increase in cumulative cultural evolution means that the knowledge necessary to be successful in modern nations and economies has moved well beyond the folk knowledge and abilities that are sufficient in traditional contexts. From this perspective, modern schooling is a massive social intervention designed to help close the gap between folk or biologically primary abilities and the biologically secondary knowledge and abilities that have accumulated over the past several millennia, especially the past few centuries (Geary, 1995, 2007). This approach laid the foundations for evolutionary educational psychology (Geary, 2002), the basic premises of which are in Table 2.

A core implication is that the child-driven activities that facilitate the development of the systems that support folk abilities will not be sufficient for the acquisition of many biological secondary abilities. This proposal is controversial and counters Rousseau's (1762/1979) child-centered argument in *Emile*, and modern versions of it (Gray, 2016). Resolution of the debate will require an understanding of the differences in the brain and cognitive mechanisms, as well as the associated activities, that facilitate folk versus academic learning (Section 3.2). The evolutionary approach also has equally important implications for understanding students' academic motivations and self-concepts (Section 4).

### 3.2 Biologically Secondary Learning

The issue here is how culturally important information is transferred from one generation to the next. For folk domains, cross-generational continuity is facilitated by built-in brain, perceptual, and cognitive scaffolds, and a motivation to engage in species-typical developmental activities. In addition, anthropologists focus on imitation and social learning for the cross-generational

**Table 2** Foundational premises of evolutionary educational psychology.

1. Hominin evolution resulted in attentional, perceptual, and cognitive systems that represent and process information in folk psychology (related to self and others), folk biology (related to other species), and folk physics (related to the physical world). There are built-in brain, perceptual, and cognitive scaffolds in these systems, but their full development requires engagement in species-typical experience-expectant activities.

2. Motivational and reward systems co-evolved with folk domains to ensure children engage in the species-typical activities that elaborate and adapt folk systems to local conditions. Adaptation to local conditions is only possible with some level of plasticity in the underlying brain systems that in turn makes them potentially modifiable for biologically secondary learning.

3. Variation in social, ecological, or climatic conditions contributed to the evolution of domain-general systems anchored in the executive attention and default mode networks. These support the generation of mental models used for step-by-step problem solving and generation of novel combinations of knowledge and technology. One result is the ability to activate aspects of folk systems from the top–down and potentially modify them without engaging the external world.

4. Scientific, technological, and academic advances emerge through interactions between folk and domain-general systems and encompass refinement of existing knowledge and technologies as well as innovation through combining existing knowledge and technologies to create qualitatively better ones. These cultural advances accumulate and result in an ever-growing gap between folk knowledge and the theories and knowledge base of the associated sciences and other disciplines (e.g., literature).

5. Schooling was developed in societies in which scientific, technological, and academic advances resulted in a gap between folk knowledge and the competencies needed for living in the society. Schools function to organize the activities of children such that they acquire the biologically secondary competencies that close the gap between folk knowledge and the occupational and social demands of the society.

6. Domain-general mechanisms and plasticity in folk domains result in the potential to modify the latter to build the biologically secondary competencies that are needed for success in modern contexts.

7. The activities that build secondary competencies often deviate from the species-typical activities that adapt folk abilities to local conditions. The result is a motivational mismatch between children's preferred activities and those that promote learning in school.

**Table 2** (cont.)

---

8. The built-in brain, perceptual, and cognitive scaffolds that guide the adaption of folk abilities to local conditions are absent for most secondary domains. Thus, these scaffolds must come from instructional materials and practices. These will often require explicit instruction, the extent to which will be a direct function of the degree to which secondary competencies differ from the supporting primary systems.

---

transfer of cultural innovations, and these are indeed important learning mechanisms. Direct and deliberate instruction of children by adults is not common in traditional societies (Lancy, 2016), although it does occur in some contexts. These include the memorization of the culture's historical narrative, common social rituals, and occasionally more specialized and complex skills, such as learning seafaring navigation (Konner, 2010). The argument here is that the rapid advances in knowledge and technology described by Lehman (1946) and others have outstripped the ability of built-in scaffolds and social learning to foster biologically secondary learning. This is especially true in scientific and technical fields, where the conceptual and mathematical knowledge needed to be successful in them has moved well beyond folk intuitions about similar phenomena, as was described for pre-Newtonian beliefs about motion. Critically, it is not just highly abstract concepts like Newton's principles of motion that are biologically secondary and difficult to learn.

Even many seemingly simple concepts are difficult to learn, like understanding that the number word "four" and the numeral "4" represent a collection of any four things, events, or actions. People in populations without formal schooling do not learn them, even though they have an intuitive sense of relative quantity; that is, they can easily distinguish between collections (e.g., fruit) that contain more or less, as long as the difference between them is not too small. This ability is an aspect of folk physics (Number in Figure 1) and is supported by the earlier mentioned approximate number system (Feigenson et al., 2004; Geary et al., 2015). The ability to discriminate smaller from larger quantities is evident in the first days of life (Mou & vanMarle, 2014), and gradually improves through childhood without instruction (Halberda & Feigenson, 2008). In contrast, it takes many months for preschool children to learn that the number word "one" refers to one and only one thing, and another six months to learn the meaning of "two" (Wynn, 1990). It is not until kindergarten or first grade that they understand that each successive number in the entire count list is one more than the number before it (e.g., "twenty-two" is one and only one more than "twenty-one") (Cheung et al., 2017).

Sometimes this conceptual knowledge emerges before children begin formal schooling, and thus it could be argued, following Rousseau (1762/1979), that children's natural activities are sufficient (Gray, 2016). There is some truth to this. There are universal biases in parent–child interactions, including children's attentiveness to and imitation of adult activities, that facilitate the transmission of cultural knowledge (Geary, 2007; Kline, 2015; Legare, 2017). The knowledge learned in this way tends to be instrumental – observable and repeatable activities resulting in a functional outcome – and focused on social conventions. This process might contribute to learning the count list (e.g., counting, "one, two, three…"), but it is not sufficient for children to learn the quantities represented by these number words (Zippert & Rittle-Johnson, 2020). Most children will learn "one" through the use of singular and plural for number words (e.g., one cat vs. two cats), but this gets them only so far (Spelke, 2017). Many children, in fact, do not learn the meaning of number words beyond "three" or "four" before they start kindergarten (Geary et al., 2019) and those who do learn it have had some type of explicit informal instruction at home that goes beyond what is typically seen in traditional contexts (Legare, 2017; LeFevre et al., 2010; Ramani et al., 2015).

In other words, some parents in WEIRD (Western, Educated, Industrialized, Rich, Democratic) societies (Henrich et al., 2010) foster their children's early academic development by engaging in activities that are similar to those found in school settings. In these cases, the early emergence of biologically secondary knowledge is not because child-centered learning in and of itself fosters this development but rather reflects the integration of school-like activities into the home environments of some children. This does not mean that children's natural behavioral biases cannot be incorporated into these school-like activities, as they likely should for young children (Geary & Berch, 2016; Toub et al., 2016). Rather, the natural activities in and of themselves are not sufficient for secondary learning.

The core questions concern the activities that promote this type of learning, wherever it occurs, and the supporting brain and cognitive systems. There are of course hundreds (if not thousands) of studies on the brain and cognitive systems that support secondary learning, such as reading and mathematics, and probably just as many on instructional approaches to this learning. With a few exceptions (Sweller et al., 2019), almost none of this research has been integrated with the evolutionary elaborations of the executive attention and default mode networks and humans' unique ability to innovate and accumulate cultural knowledge across generations.

### 3.2.1 Brain and Cognitive Mechanisms

It has been known for well over a century that people who do well on one type of perceptual, cognitive, or academic task generally do well on other such tasks, which led Spearman (1904, p. 285) to conclude "that all branches of intellectual activity have in common one fundamental function (or group of functions)." Spearman termed the fundamental function or group of functions general intelligence, although it is sometimes called general ability (the apex of Figure 5). The latter is easily measured by various cognitive tests, and performance on these is predictive of myriad outcomes in the modern world, including performance in school and on the job (Hunter, & Schmidt, 1996; Kriegbaum et al., 2018; Lubinski, 2000; Walberg, 1984; Wolfram, 2023). As mentioned, general ability can be understood at multiple levels of analysis, from cellular functions to cognitive processes. The latter and the underlying brain networks are the most relevant to learning in school and therefore the focus here.

Working memory and broader executive functions are the focus of much of the cognitive research on general ability, which in turn supports the problem solving that is central to fluid intelligence (Demetriou et al., 2014; Engle et al., 1999; Mackintosh & Bennett, 2003; Redick et al., 2016; Unsworth et al., 2014). The central cognitive processes are debated, but a strong contender is executive attention, that is, the "capacity whereby memory representations are maintained in a highly active state in the presence of interference" (Kane & Engle, 2002, p. 638). In other words, it is the ability to maintain top–down attentional control during learning or problem-solving episodes. Kane and Engle's proposal was developed based on a substantial body of empirical research (e.g., Engle et al., 1999; Burgoyne & Engle, 2020), but without consideration of the evolutionary origins of this ability. As described in Section 2.2.4, brain systems that support top–down attentional control have undergone modification during human evolution which resulted in competencies that far exceed those found in great apes. Top–down attentional control also supports the generation of mental models and use of the working memory resources needed to evaluate the likely outcomes of alternative scenarios in the context of these models (Geary, 2005).

Critically, research studies on the brain systems that support general ability have identified these same evolutionarily modified networks, especially the prefrontal and parietal executive attention networks (Barbey, 2018; Basten et al., 2015; Jung & Haier, 2007). Jung and Haier's classic review of brain imaging studies identified areas of the prefrontal cortex (e.g., areas 9, 10, 47, Figure 6), parietal cortex (e.g., areas 40, 7), and the anterior cingulate (area 32) as often engaged when people solve complex cognitive problems. The exact constellation of engaged brain regions and their dynamic interactions will depend on the specific problem-solving tasks and demands used during the brain imagining study, but the fronto-parietal and salience (including the anterior cingulate) networks are typically engaged (Santarnecchi et al., 2017), as will the cingulo-opercular network if the task demands continual alertness (Coste & Kleinschmidt, 2016).

The core issues concern how attention-driven focus changes the brain and results in learning, and how these mechanisms might differ for evolutionarily privileged folk abilities and evolutionarily novel biologically secondary abilities. Generally, the full development of both primary and secondary abilities will require experience-driven activation of the supporting brain areas and networks, which results in gray (e.g., changes in neurons or supporting cells) and white matter (e.g., enhanced myelinization) changes that support enhanced competencies (Zatorre et al., 2012). Plasticity occurs at multiple levels, from molecular changes in synaptic functions to synchronization of large-scale brain networks, but the focus here is on small- and large-scale networks (Barbey, 2018; Power et al., 2013).

My proposal is that primary folk abilities are privileged because the organization of the brain systems that support them are at least partially inherent, including small-scale networks that are pretuned to process evolutionarily salient information (e.g., speech sounds) and large-scale networks that integrate them into functional competencies (e.g., language). Inherent motivational and reward systems result in behavioral biases that create species-typical experiences and attendant activation of these same systems. The activation fine-tunes small-scale networks to local conditions and solidifies their organization into large-scale networks. Secondary abilities do not have these scaffolds and behavioral biases and thus top–down attentional control is relatively more important for their acquisition than it is for primary abilities. Examples of secondary learning are provided later, and an illustration of primary scaffolds in the next section. The approach here seems to leave the default mode network out in the cold, as engagement of attentional networks for secondary learning typically inhibits DMN activity (e.g., Howard-Jones et al., 2016). Nevertheless, the DMN has been implicated in creativity and innovation, as mentioned earlier, and is important for noncognitive aspects of school learning, such as academic self-efficacy and self-esteem (Geary & Xu, 2022; Yeshurun et al., 2021), discussed in Section 4.2.

### 3.2.2 Scaffolds for Primary Abilities

Inherent brain networks are organized as small-scale intramodular neural communication systems with long-distance intermodular neural connections (Barbey, 2018; Power et al., 2013). Increases in local intramodular connectivity and connections between physically close local networks (i.e., close brain regions) support fine-grain processing of information (Kaas, 1982), whereas long-distance white matter connections integrate modules to form a functional brain network and cognitive competency. Some of the components of these networks are also parts of multiple networks (called hubs) and thus can be engaged across different types of cognitive demands or tasks. There are large-scale networks, such as the default mode network, that serve multiple, often domain-general functions (Yeo et al., 2011), as well as smaller-scale domain-specific networks that can result from learning or inherent biases and engagement in species-typical activities. The latter are not as well understood as the large-scale networks (e.g., attentional, DMN), but there is evidence for networks that support several of the earlier described folk abilities, including language (Gernsbacher & Kaschak, 2003), theory of mind (Schurz et al., 2014), spatial navigation (Herbet & Duffau, 2020), and mechanical reasoning/tool use (Frey, 2008; Hegarty, 2004). Note that subregions of many of these networks might also be engaged in multiple other networks, but still show unique patterns of synchronized activity across distributed brain regions that support folk abilities, such as theory of mind (Herbet & Duffau, 2020).

Language provides an example of a folk network, inherent scaffolds, and plasticity. One component of the network, the planum temporale (part of Wernicke's area, Figure 6), is a small-scale module that is especially sensitive to the acoustic features of human language sounds and is integrated with Broca's area, among others. The latter is often considered a language-specific area, but in fact has both domain-general and language-specific functions (Matchin, 2018). The domain-general components include its contributions to verbal working memory (e.g., trying to maintain a new phone number in short-term memory) and the language-specific functions include retrieving word and sentence meanings, providing structure (syntax) to and activating language sounds that are important for comprehending and producing speech. The language-specific components of Broca's area generally show synchronized co-activation with more distant areas that support the processing of language sounds (e.g., planum temporale), contribute to their comprehension, and help their articulation when spoken (Fedorenko & Blank, 2020). This integrated brain network supports language production and comprehension and, with instruction, reading and writing.

Small-scale local intramodular systems, such as the planum temporale, often show experience-dependent plasticity. Plasticity is a common feature of the mammalian cortex and involves the development of more neurons and connections among them than will ultimately be needed (Faust et al., 2021). As an example, human infants are sensitive to all naturally produced human language sounds (phonemes), including those that are not part of their parents' native language. Over the course of the first year of life, they become more sensitive to the language sounds they regularly hear (activity-dependent strengthening of the corresponding cell networks) and lose sensitivity to language sounds they have not heard (Kuhl et al., 1997). The neurons, axons, and synapses that supported the latter are pruned; that is, they largely disappear, which reduces the energetic cost of the system. In this example, the pruning fine-tunes a basic component of the language system such that it is better adapted to current conditions through engagement in species-typical activities (e.g., parent–infant interactions). This form of intramodular plasticity opens the door for adaptation (within limits) for processing evolutionarily novel information (Section 3.2.3).

Large-scale functional networks begin to emerge during prenatal brain development (Schöpf et al., 2012; Turk et al., 2019). These are identified through patterns of spontaneous activity while the fetus is at rest and result in activity patterns that will integrate and strengthen the connections among the smaller-scale modules that are components of large-scale networks. The basic architecture of the language system is one of the networks that begins to develop prenatally. The basic architecture of this network, including the basic structure of Broca's and Wernicke's areas, emerge by the end of the second trimester along with the subcortical areas involved in processing sounds (Ghio et al., 2021). The white matter connections between these areas are also emerging at this time and continue to develop through the third trimester and undergo strengthening and refinement through adolescence (Hagmann et al., 2010). Much of this development is driven by genes and inputs from subcortical regions (e.g., Grasby et al., 2020), with the latter resulting in activity-dependent strengthening of cortical language areas, in keeping with the protocortex hypothesis (O'Leary et al., 1994). The combination of prenatal development of core features of the language system and the bias for infants and parents to engage in social interactions that create further co-activation of this network strengthens it and supports the full emergence of language competencies.

### 3.2.3 Examples of Secondary Learning: Reading

The language system illustrates an inherent scaffold that supports the emergence of a folk ability and at the same time illustrates intramodular plasticity and the importance of integrating modules into networks. As mentioned, intramodular plasticity provides a window for an experience-dependent coaxing of these areas to process evolutionarily novel information, as illustrated with learning how to read. White matter connectivity also shows some degree of plasticity that facilitates the integration of physically distant modules in potentially novel ways. The white matter connections between areas that will eventually support secondary abilities are largely preexisting for a different function, but these can be strengthened and repurposed with instruction (Yeatman et al., 2012). As described, the fine-tuning and normal development of many primary folk systems requires activity-dependent co-activation of the underlying brain areas, and this activation automatically results from built-in behavioral biases that create species-typical experiences (Figure 2).

Cognitive and brain imaging studies confirm that these species-typical experiences are not sufficient for the development of reading skills. Rather, instruction must focus attention (e.g., on letters, words) in ways that do not typically occur. The fronto-parietal and other attentional networks are critical to this process (Barbey, 2018; Geary, 2007, 2008), and when they are disengaged, the default mode network becomes active and results in self-referential mind wandering instead of attentiveness to academic material (Betzel et al., 2016). Critically, the top–down focus of attention can contribute to the modification of brain areas such that they process novel information (e.g., words, sentences) and solidify the integration of these modified regions into functional biologically secondary networks (e.g., fluent reading). In other words, top–down attentional control can prime the development of unique configurations (within limits that are not currently well understood) of activated brain areas that are not evolutionarily privileged and would not occur through engagement in species-typical activities.

Bassett et al. (2011) demonstrated as much by showing that visual–motor learning (similar to reading musical notes and playing on a piano) resulted in novel configurations of visual and motor modules that stabilized overtime time and predicted subsequent performance. Changes such as these occur through a remodeling of the connectome, that is, the physical mechanisms that link together neurons and networks of neurons. The process can occur through changes in synaptic connections between individual neurons, changes in the density or configuration of intramodular connections (these can be gains or losses of connections), or changes in the efficiency of long-range white matter intermodular connections (Bennett et al., 2018). The latter occurs through changes in the myelin covering of axons, which in turn improve speed of neural transmission and contribute to ease of synchronizing integrated modules and solidifying them (Sampaio-Baptista & Johansen-Berg, 2017).

The development of reading skills illustrates how a combination of top–down attentional focus and instruction can modify primary systems to create an evolutionarily novel academic ability. Reading instruction essentially opens a door to the evolved language and several other folk-psychological abilities; theory of mind, for instance, would support understanding a fictional character's goals and intentions in the context of a written story. Prior studies have confirmed a substantive overlap between the brain areas and systems that support language and those that support basic reading competencies, including phonological decoding (sounding out letters and words), reading fluency, and text comprehension (Paulesu et al., 2001; Price & Mechelli, 2005; Pugh et al., 1997; Turkeltaub et al., 2003). It has also been long recognized that reading and writing are built onto the evolved language system (Mann, 1984; Rozin, 1976).

More recently, brain imaging studies have provided insights into how the melding of reading and language occurs. Orthography, or the translation of letters and words into sounds, is reading's gateway into the language system. The first steps to building this gateway include an explicit awareness of distinct language sounds, that is, phonemic awareness, and the ability to decode unfamiliar written words into these basic sounds. Decoding requires an explicit representation of the sound (e.g., *ba*, *da*, *ka*) in verbal working memory and the association of this sound and blends of sounds with corresponding visual patterns, specifically letters (e.g., *b*, *d*, *k*) and letter combinations (Bradley & Bryant, 1983). Verbal working memory is integrated with the language system and has been proposed as a mechanism that supports language comprehension and early vocabulary acquisition (Baddeley et al., 1998; Matchin, 2018; Mann, 1984). Unlike the initial stages of learning to read and comprehend written words, natural word learning occurs quickly (sometimes with one exposure), and the associated mechanisms operate implicitly, that is, without effortful top–down engagement of the attention networks (Lenneberg, 1969; Pinker, 1994). In other words, even though most of the same brain systems are involved in learning the meaning of spoken words and understanding these same words during the act of reading, the former occurs without instruction and the latter will not occur without instruction.

Yarkoni et al.'s (2008) brain imaging study of story reading confirmed engagement of the traditional language system, as well as an area of the brain called the visual word form area (VWFA; McCandliss et al., 2003). The VWFA is located in the fusiform gyrus, which spans parts of the ventral (bottom) occipital and temporal cortices (BA 37, Figure 6). The integration of reading with the language system capitalizes on preexisting white matter connections between the area that will eventually become the VWFA and the language areas (Bouhali et al., 2014; Saygin et al., 2016). Saygin et al. determined that the area that will become (with instruction) the VWFA does not respond to letters or words for children who have not yet learned how to read, indicating it is not inherently biased to process letters and words. Li et al. (2020) confirmed that this part of the fusiform gyrus is integrated with the language system in newborns, and Chen et al. (2019) showed extensive connectivity to parts of the fronto-parietal attention network, particularly those related to top–down attentional control, visuospatial working memory, and control of eye movements. The integration of the area that will become the VWFA with the attentional and language systems supports the ability to verbally describe the details of objects that are the focus of attention, which might be its evolved function.

In this view, learning how to read modifies a subset of cells that would typically (without instruction) process features of objects (e.g., shape, angle) such that this network of cells becomes sensitive to features of letters and words, reflecting some degree of intramodular plasticity (Dehaene et al., 2010). The preexisting integration of this network of cells with the top–down attentional control system supports the disciplined visual scanning needed to learn to read and during the act of reading, and enables the translation of the visual patterns (i.e., written words) into language sounds. Engaging in reading and related activities (e.g., sounding out words) results in experience-dependent activation of the VWFA and these preexisting white matter connections, which appears to increase the myelination of these connections and solidifies the network (Dehaene et al., 2010; Moulton et al., 2019; Stevens et al., 2017). The result is a highly specialized intermodular biologically secondary network that supports reading and writing.

These studies also indicate that humans (or any other species) would not have the ability to create writing systems or learn to read without plasticity in the area that supports the VWFA and without the preexisting integration of this area with the attentional and language systems. The complexity of the language system and the reading system built upon it creates multiple opportunities for difficulties with reading and in extreme cases dyslexia, that is, difficulties with reading despite adequate instruction and cognitive ability (e.g., Nicolson & Fawcett, 2019; Stanovich, 1988). Difficulties in phonological processing, that is, with discriminating and processing specific language sounds (e.g., *ba*, *pa*), results in a compromised ability to sound out or decode words and to build fluency in processing word sounds (Stanovich, 1988). Not surprisingly, the VWFA is implicated in some cases of dyslexia, whereby the area has not become as specialized for processing words as it is with typical readers (Brem et al., 2020; Richlan et al., 2011). This could be due to general deficits in processing object details, in which case reading difficulties would co-occur with deficits in processing the details of other images. It could also be due to relatively poor attentional focus during the early stages of letter and word learning such that the VWFA does not become as adapted to word processing as it is for other readers; in this case, poor reading would co-occur with broader attentional difficulties such as attention deficit and hyperactivity disorder.

In any case, the development of writing systems and the ability to learn to read and write is a relatively straightforward example of adapting primary systems to create an evolutionarily novel academic ability, as the primary systems are pre-adapted for reading and writing. The pre-adaptation is not any type of evolutionary foresight (Gould & Vrba, 1982), but once the system was in place, the potential to develop writing systems emerged but lay dormant for 200,000 or so years.

### 3.2.4 Examples of Secondary Learning: Mathematics

Mathematics represents a more complex system of biologically secondary knowledge than does reading and writing. The field emerged over the course of several thousand years through the efforts of numerous individuals (Dantzig, 1930), and is composed of increasingly (across grades) complex procedures for operating on representations of quantities and increasingly abstract concepts. As with reading, there may be pre-adaptions that facilitate some aspects of mathematics learning, including a sensitivity to relative quantity (Number, Figure 1) and an implicit understanding of the properties of objects and the geometry of the physical world. Even so, the relation between these primary folk abilities and an explicit understanding of number, arithmetic, geometry, and other mathematical areas is debated and not well understood.

At a general level and in keeping with the development of reading and writing competencies, multiple brain areas are engaged during mathematical learning and problem solving and their repeated co-activation results in the consolidation of biologically secondary functional networks that support mathematics skills and knowledge (Amalric & Dehaene, 2018; Menon & Chang, 2021). The initial learning and associated co-activation of these networks is driven by the top–down attentional control networks, and as these math-specific networks strengthen engagement of the attentional networks declines (Rivera et al., 2005).

The foundation stone for math-specific networks is laid with the building of a visual number form area analogous to and situated near the VWFA and with inherent connections to the approximate number system, language network (left hemisphere), and the attentional control networks (Yeo et al., 2020). As with letters and words, there is no inherent bias to process numerals (e.g., 7, 381), and thus this area has to be built with repeated exposure to them. Amalric and Dehaene (2018) found that the areas involved in processing numerals are also engaged when professional mathematicians process more complex mathematical symbols, suggesting that with sufficient practice areas of the temporal-occipital (fusiform gyrus) cortex (segment of area 37, Figure 6) automatically process meaningful mathematical information (e.g., algebraic identities, $(a + b)^2 = a^2 + b^2 + 2ab$).

As described, the development of a VWFA provides access to a ready-made system of folk abilities that support reading fluency and comprehension. The link between the number form area and the ANS and integrated spatial areas of the parietal cortex is analogous in some ways to the reading-language link, but not in a way that can fully explain the learning of biologically secondary mathematics. To be sure, there is substantive evidence for an evolved sensitivity to the relative quantities of collections of objects, which is found in human infants (e.g., Mou & vanMarle, 2014) and many other species ranging from insects to apes (for reviews see Feigenson et al., 2004; Geary et al., 2015). The evolutionary advantages include more efficient foraging (Gallistel, 1990) and predator avoidance (predation risks are reduced if one joins a larger group). Whatever the evolutionary selection pressures, it is possible that the ANS is part of the evolutionary foundation for the building of explicit mathematical knowledge and concepts, but how this might occur is debated and not as straightforward as the language–reading link (Mussolin et al., 2016; Szkudlarek & Brannon, 2017; Szűcs & Myers, 2017).

One difference is a more direct relation between reading and language than between mathematics and the ANS. Consider that the sentence "The dog chased the cat" sounds the same and means the same whether it is spoken or read from a story. The ANS in comparison represents approximate quantities that are arrayed along a mental number line (Dehaene et al., 2003). The neural representation of individual quantities, such as five, is fuzzy in the ANS but precise in mathematics. Similarly, the array of quantities from smaller to larger on the mental number line does not precisely map to the mathematical number line (Dehaene et al., 2003). The parietal brain areas (i.e., intraparietal sulcus and adjacent areas, bottom of area 7, Figure 6) that process quantities along the mental number line show sharper distinctions between 1 and 2 than between 21 and 22 (Dehaene et al., 2003), whereas the mathematical difference between these two pairs is identical (i.e., 1). In other words, there is not a one-to-one relation between the inherent ways in which the ANS represents quantities and possibly operations on them (e.g., combining two sets) and the corresponding properties of formal mathematics (Gallistel & Gelman, 2000; Hubbard et al., 2005).

One possibility is that the ANS is recycled or adapted through instruction to form accurate representations of symbolic quantities (e.g., numerals), their relations, and other mathematical knowledge (Dehaene & Cohen, 2007). A form of adaptation does occur, as described, for the VWFA and the number form area, but this is not happening in the ANS in the same way. To be sure, brain imaging studies have shown that determining the magnitudes represented by Arabic numerals and solving arithmetic problems engages the ANS

(Cohen Kadosh et al., 2011; Piazza et al., 2007; Rivera et al., 2005), and performance on ANS tasks is consistently correlated with mathematics achievement (Feigenson et al., 2013; Geary & vanMarle, 2016; Libertus et al., 2011).

However, engagement of these areas does not necessarily mean that the ANS is supporting the processing of mathematics symbols and knowledge in the same way that engagement of the language system supports the act of reading and reading comprehension. As noted, there is not a one-to-one correspondence between the inherent structure of the mental number line and the mathematical number line. Early studies showed that children's initial placements of numerals (e.g., 21 on a 0 to 100 number line) on a physical number line followed the predicted ANS pattern (i.e., separation of smaller numbers and compression of larger ones), and with schooling, these placements corresponded to the structure of the mathematical number line (Siegler & Braithwaite, 2017; Siegler & Opfer, 2003). An early argument was that these education-driven changes resulted from changes in the structure of the mental number line such that it mirrored the linear mathematical line (Dehaene et al., 2008). The direct formation of extensive linear representations is unlikely, however, as this would involve more precise numeral-to-magnitude mappings than can be supported by the ANS. Moreover, the ANS does not appear to support fractional representations and does not support representations of negative numbers, and thus it is unclear how children would learn these magnitudes and where they are situated on the mathematical number line.

An alternative is that the ANS provides an intuitive understanding of less to more along a mental number line, and this provides a basic structural or conceptual scaffold for building a mathematical number line through instruction. This type of structure mapping maintains the visuospatial representation of the number line and engages the inherent bias to represent features of the world along a magnitude-based continuum but does not require the formation of precise one-to-one mappings of numerals or fraction magnitudes to the ANS (Carey, 2009; Sullivan & Barner, 2014). In other words, the inherent contributions to number line learning are in the inherent bias to represent magnitudes along a single continuous dimension that often has a spatial component to it (Summerfield et al., 2020), and this is the primary conceptual scaffold that enables the explicit construction of the mathematical number line. The linking of this primary magnitude-continuum scaffold in the ANS to symbolic number sequences (i.e., counting sequence, number line) is experience-dependent and facilitated by the hippocampus (area 35, Figure 6) and angular gyrus (area 39; Wagner & Rusconi, 2023), both of which are involved in early mathematics learning (e.g., Castaldi et al., 2020; Menon & Chang, 2021;Qin et al., 2014) and more generally to concept formation (Davis & Yee, 2019; Zeithamova et al., 2019).

Learning thus involves the experience-dependent integration of these brain regions which are then dynamically engaged when students situate numerals on a physical number line rather than reading off the positions from the ANS. To perform well on the mathematical number line, students need to explicitly understand the formal mathematical properties of the line, which then guides their placements during the act of positioning numerals on the line (Dotan & Dehaene, 2016; Kim & Opfer, 2018). Such a dynamic process allows for strategic or contextual influences on number line performance based on students' conceptual understanding of numeral magnitudes, above and beyond an influence of the ANS (Barth & Paladino, 2011; Cohen & Blanc-Goldhammer, 2011; Rouder & Geary, 2014; Slusser et al., 2013). For instance, a concept-based structure mapping and an explicit understanding of the properties of the mathematical number line would allow students to locate the midpoint on a 0 to 100 line and use this and the endpoints to place numerals (e.g., 37, 91) in the correct position; a similar process of breaking the line into segments to facilitate placements occurs for students who are learning the fractions number line (Siegler et al., 2011). The conceptual complexity of the mathematical number line increases further with the introduction of negative numbers; this conceptual complexity might be why the line as we know it today was not fully integrated into mathematics until the seventeenth century (Danzig, 1930; Núñez, 2008).

Visuospatial abilities also contribute to students' understanding of the ordinal relations among numerals and number words (e.g., 3 > 2) and accuracy in placing them on the mathematical number line (Geary et al., 2021; Longo & Lourenco, 2007; Zorzi et al., 2002). In fact, there is a well-documented relation between visuospatial abilities and learning and performance in many areas of mathematics (Atit et al., 2022; Casey & Ganley, 2021; Geary et al., 2023; Hawes & Ansari, 2020; Mix, 2019), but the ways in which these abilities influence mathematics learning are not well understood. From an evolutionary perspective, the visuospatial systems that support navigation and object processing might, in theory, facilitate the learning of corresponding aspects of mathematics just as the smaller-to-large organization of the ANS provides an intuitive understanding of the basic structure of the mathematical number line.

Infants' behavior indicates that their perceptual systems are sensitive to features of object shape, such as edges and angles, which in turn provides a sense of object continuity across time and space (Newcombe et al., 2013; Slater et al., 1990; Spelke et al., 2010). The systems that support navigation, such as the hippocampus (area 35, Figure 6), generate a cognitive map that includes Euclidean features of the real world, such as distance and angular relations between objects in the ecology (Milner & Goodale, 1995; O'Keefe & Nadel, 1978). The issue is whether this implicit understanding of objects and navigation provides ready-made basic knowledge of the properties of geometric objects and the basics of formal Euclidean geometry (Geary, 1995; Spelke et al., 2010); objects do not have the abstract features of geometric shapes (e.g., smooth face and edges), but the underlying system supports thinking about objects in abstract form. If so, the instructional key would be to build a bridge to this knowledge like the VWFA provides a bridge to the language system. Unfortunately, this does not appear to be the case: Children do not automatically engage their navigational or object-processing systems during formal geometry tasks, even when there is a clear mapping between these visuospatial representations and the geometry tasks (Dillon et al., 2013).

These results, however, are not the same as saying that different brain systems support primary navigation abilities and formal Euclidean geometry or object processing and an understanding of the properties of solids. As with language and the development of writing systems, humans could not have discovered these aspects of mathematics without brain systems for processing object features and navigating in large-scale space that are integrated with the top–down attentional control networks that support explicit problem solving. The critical difference is that knowledge of these features of the world is *implicit* (people are not consciously aware of them) in the organization of the associated brain, perceptual, and cognitive systems, whereas the corresponding mathematical knowledge is hard-won (often emerging after centuries of work and debate), *explicit*, and objectively defined based on mathematical principles. The knowledge is represented in ways – written, mathematical, visually – that can be communicated with and understood by other people and that becomes part of the earlier described cumulative culture. In other words, mathematicians discovered these features of mathematics through goal-directed hard work, supported by the attentional control systems, and were able to visualize and think about the mathematical properties of objects, for example, because there are folk systems for processing features of real-world objects.

As one last consideration, let us return to Einstein's mental simulations, that is, the use of attention-driven mental models for problem solving. In his case and with others during the general development of mathematics as a field, the simulations are goal directed and likely involve alterations between engagement of the default mode network for the generation of ideas (e.g., forming associations between remotely related concepts) and the top–down attentional control systems for the subsequent explicit evaluations, refinements, and syntheses of these ideas. Indeed, this process is consistent with Hadamard's (1945) analysis of how mathematicians make their discoveries, more general analyses of the processes that underlie creative contributions (Simonton, 2003), and extends to discoveries in other technical fields (e.g., Kell et al., 2013). In the case of mathematics, the simulations often have a visual (e.g., imagining a geometric solid) or more dynamic visuospatial component to them, as described by Einstein.

In educational settings, students often use these types of simulations for mathematical problem solving, as in solving word problems; performance on these problems is predictive of later economic and educational outcomes, controlling other factors (e.g., general ability; Park et al., 2007; Rivera-Batiz, 1992). As with most problems, multistep mathematics word problems can be solved in multiple ways, one of which involves the generation of a mental model that includes a visuospatial representation of the relations described in the problem (Casey & Ganley, 2021; Lewis & Mayer, 1987). The generation requires constructing a visual or physical sketch of the relations in the problem, and this in turn helps the problem solver to better understand these relations and reduces problem-solving errors (Jitendra & Woodward, 2019; Lewis, 1989). The generation of these mental models, however, does not come naturally for the solving of mathematical word problems – many students do not generate useful models and those who do often require some type of instruction (Lewis, 1989; van Garderen et al., 2013). Instruction in this view is not only teaching the mathematical content but also how to co-opt these folk systems (visuospatial and mental models in this example) to better understand this content and to problem solve using the rules of mathematics (e.g., Ünal et al., 2023).

In summary, modern mathematics is an evolutionarily novel academic domain that emerged over several millennia, and thus there is no reason to believe that people have an intuitive understanding of much of it. The ANS is the closest folk ability to modern mathematics, but even here only provides an intuitive understanding that relative magnitudes can be arrayed from smaller to larger, and perhaps a basic ability to combine them. While this might provide a general conceptual structure for understanding symbolic quantities, the number line, and perhaps basic arithmetic, the more precise properties of numbers (e.g., negative numbers, irrationals), the mathematical number line, and symbolic arithmetic are biologically secondary knowledge and emerged fitfully during the development of mathematics as an academic field. As a result, it is not surprising that it takes years of instruction for students to acquire this knowledge – their intuitive understanding of quantities and continuous magnitudes is nowhere near sufficient for this knowledge to emerge without extensive instruction (Siegler & Braithwaite, 2017).

## 4 Noncognitive Processes and Educational Outcomes

There are several noncognitive factors that contribute to various academic outcomes, including aspects of personality, self-concepts, and affective or emotional factors such as mathematics and test anxiety. The relation between these traits and academic outcomes is well established but has not been integrated into an evolutionary approach to learning. Thus, the goal here is to provide an initial discussion as to how they might be incorporated into this approach. At a general level, these noncognitive processes must operate by influencing engagement of the top–down attentional systems that support secondary learning. These processes can involve the here-and-now ability to maintain attentional focus during learning episodes and maintain goals that enable a long-term investment in schooling. Both the short-term processes and the long-term goal maintenance are likely supported, at least in part, by the evolutionary changes in the top–down attentional networks, that is, the ability to override prepotent biases (e.g., to socialize) and stay focused on less compelling activities, such as learning mathematics (Csikszentmihalyi & Hunter, 2003; Geary, 1995). The evolutionary elaboration of the default mode network supports the ability to imagine future states and thus understand the long-term benefits of schooling. The DMN also contributes to self-awareness, which in turn sets the foundation for the development of academic self-concepts (Geary & Xu, 2022).

## 4.1 Conscientiousness and Anxiety

We begin with conscientiousness, which is the one component of personality that is consistently related to academic and occupational outcomes (Schneider & Preckel, 2017). It reflects general organizational and planning skills, a preference for order and routine in daily activities, and more generally a self-controlled future orientation (Costantini & Perugini, 2016). Among other things, conscientiousness contributes to grade-point average across the elementary school years and into college, although some other aspects of personality (e.g., social agreeableness) are also important in earlier grades (Poropat, 2009). Moreover, conscientiousness is unrelated (or slightly negatively correlated) to general ability (Anglim et al., 2022), and thus contributes to educational outcomes in ways that differ from the direct contributions of the fronto-parietal network.

The core facets of contentiousness that contribute to educational outcomes are self-control and the ability to maintain a focus on long-term goals, especially maintaining goal-focused behaviors (e.g., studying) for activities that are not particularly interesting (Spielmann et al., 2022). The core – self-controlled future orientation – of conscientiousness is consistent with the earlier described use of mental models for problem solving and mental time travel. In other words, the core of conscientiousness might reflect a component of this recently evolved system – specifically, a component that maintains focus on long-term goals and involves the suppression of potential distractors that would deflect from achieving these goals. The brain systems underlying conscientiousness are not fully understood but overlap with the salience network (Rueter et al., 2018; Sassenberg et al., 2023; S. Wang et al., 2019; Yi et al., 2023). Recall, this network is important for switching between the fronto-parietal and default mode networks and is involved in management of motivational and affective states (Menon & Uddin, 2010; Schimmelpfennig et al., 2023). From this perspective, conscientiousness might reflect, in part, the ability to maintain engagement of the fronto-parietal network (through the salience network) during learning episodes and to engage components of the DMN that support the generation of future states, including long-term educational goals.

The management of affective states comes through the integration of the salience network with the emotion-processing amygdala (area 25, Figure 6). One evolved function of the amygdala is to detect threat and thus is related to ease of forming phobias associated with evolutionarily relevant contexts (e.g., presence of a predator) (Öhman & Mineka, 2001; Seligman, 1971). The amygdala also contributes to the formation of fears associated with evolutionarily novel or seemingly nonthreatening objects or situations (McNally, 1987). The latter is common across species and provides a form of plasticity for adapting to new threats in the environment. For some students these systems are engaged in educational settings and can result in anxiety for certain academic topics or testing situations.

The phenomena can be illustrated with mathematics anxiety, that is, apprehension or anxiety when having to engage with mathematics and especially mathematics tests (Ashcraft, 2002; Baloglu & Koçak, 2006; Hembree, 1990). Higher mathematics anxiety is associated with lower mathematics achievement and avoidance of mathematics coursework (Caviola et al., 2022; Dowker et al., 2016; Ma, 1999), but the cause–effect relation is unclear. Generally, lower mathematics achievement is associated with later increases in mathematics anxiety (Geary et al., 2023; Ma & Xu, 2004), suggesting that difficulties with mathematics and the need to continually engage with it during schooling can result in a learned fear or anxiety. In this view, mathematics anxiety emerges through fear conditioning, whereby anxiety-prone individuals are more likely to acquire it than their calmer peers if they experience anxiety during mathematics learning (e.g., through interactions with math anxious teachers) or evaluations (Levine & Pantoja, 2021). Indeed, individuals with high levels of math anxiety have physiological and other responses like those found with phobias (Hembree, 1990; Lyons & Beilock, 2012), and the genetic risks associated with general anxiety contribute to mathematics anxiety, independent of math competencies (Wang et al., 2014).

These patterns are consistent with Young et al.'s (2012) finding that mathematics anxiety is correlated with engagement of an amygdala nucleus that contributes to fear conditioning (i.e., reacting with anxiety to cues of potential threats). In these situations, the anxiety-provoking situation engages the salience network that in turn can result in an exaggerated focus on and response to the potential threat. This shift in focus (e.g., ruminating on potentially failing) disrupts the attentional engagement needed for learning episodes and through this can interfere with performance on mathematics tests or learning (Ashcraft & Krause, 2007; G. Ramirez et al., 2018). Pletzer et al. (2015) found that individuals with higher levels of mathematics anxiety showed less deactivation of the default mode network than their peers when engaged in number processing. The poor deactivation of the DMN is in keeping with a self-relevant preoccupation during mathematics activities and will interfere with mathematics learning and performance.

More generally, many people cope with these reactions by avoiding the situations associated with the fear or anxiety, which perpetuates it (McNally, 1987). Avoidance of mathematics will reduce long-term educational and occupational options, and thus reductions in anxiety could be beneficial for many students. A common approach is to increase exposure to the threat, which over time can result in a decline in the associated fear or anxiety. For mathematics this would involve improving basic mathematics competencies, starting at a level that would ensure success, which has been found to simultaneously reduce mathematics anxiety and reduce the overreactivity of the amygdala (Supekar et al., 2015). Other components of such interventions might involve changing how students appraise their difficulties with mathematics – specifically, instilling a realization that occasional struggles are due to the difficulty of learning the material and not due to lack of ability to improve one's mathematical competencies (G. Ramirez et al., 2018).

In any event, the gist of this section and the former one is that the core noncognitive factors (more below) that influence educational outcomes are related, at least in part, to the evolutionary elaboration of the earlier described brain networks (Section 2.2), including the salience network and components of the default mode network. Recall that the key to building secondary brain networks is experience-dependent activation of the network of regions that support secondary abilities. The salience network is important here for balancing the activation of the fronto-parietal and DMN networks and maintaining engagement of the former during academic learning or performance episodes. Although the DMN is typically active when attention is unfocused, it can be engaged from the top–down when recalling past personal experiences (episodic memory) and for generating mental models of potential future states. The important component here is the generation of long-term educational goals (e.g., imagining oneself as a college graduate) and maintaining focus on these goals. The construction of strategies to reduce the difference between one's current state and the desired future state, such as obstacles to achieving educational goals, likely engages the fronto-parietal network.

## 4.2 Self-Awareness and Academic Self-Concepts

The evolutionary elaboration of the default mode network and the resulting ability to generate self-referential thoughts and mental models was likely driven by a within-species arms race focused on status climbing and resource control (Garin et al., 2022; Geary, 2005). These mechanisms did not evolve to support academic learning, but they do contribute to innovation in secondary domains and the ability to build mental models for academic problem solving. The focus here is on the associated ability to engage in top–down self-reflections or self-awareness, which is the "ability to take oneself as the object of attention and thought" (Leary & Buttermore, 2003, p. 366), and the generation of a self-schema (Figure 1). The latter is knowledge that contributes to a social identity, as well as self-knowledge related to traits that are socially and culturally important, including academic self-concepts (Geary & Xu, 2022). An evolutionary perspective on these issues helps to explain some perplexing findings, such as why many people are more focused on their physical than academic traits, even though educational outcomes are strongly related to success in the modern world. The perspective also highlights the importance of a cultural focus on academic traits, that is, that gaining them is socially valued.

We begin by stepping back and considering various forms of self-awareness and their evolution. One influential proposal includes five forms of self-knowledge (Neisser, 1988). The first two are *ecological* and *interpersonal*, which do not involve an explicit reflection on the self and ecological and social interactions, just coherent self-interested and species-typical responses to these contexts, as illustrated by synchronous mother–infant interactions (Bernieri et al., 1988). The *private self* is a conscious ability to remember events that are only available to the self, but supports the ability to convey internal states (e.g., hunger) to others and may have contributed to the evolution of theory of mind (Gallup, 1998). The *extended self* and the *conceptual self* are the most highly developed in humans relative to other species (Leary & Buttermore,

2003). The extended self is an awareness of self-continuity across time and integrates past, present, and potential future representations of oneself, contributing to the maintenance of long-term goals. The conceptual self is composed of more abstract representations of the self, such as social identity (e.g., as a student), personality (e.g., conscientious), and common ways of responding (e.g., punctual).

People identify social relationships as a core part of the self-schema or conceptual self (Esnaola et al., 2020; Harter, 2006; Shavelson et al., 1976). Physical abilities and physical appearance are also important components of self-concept, which is consistent with an evolutionary perspective. In traditional contexts, physical abilities are important for survival-related activities (e.g., hunting) and reproductive competition, especially for men, whereas physical appearance influences mate choices and general social treatment (Geary, 2021). The importance of social relationships and physical traits for the development of one's self-concept is likely a human universal and contributes to pride or self-esteem (Durkee et al., 2019) and is thus supported by inherent motivational and reward systems (e.g., feeling good after socializing). At the same time, plasticity in the formation of self-concepts and the differential valuation of them is expected from an evolutionary perspective, given the many ecological and social niches occupied by humans. Indeed, ethnographies indicate that prestige and self-esteem are related to success in culturally important endeavors, including farming skills in horticulturalists, animal husbandry in pastoralists, and fighting competencies in groups in conflict (Barkow, 1975). Self-concepts in these culturally relevant areas can be important for developing a specialized niche within these contexts based on self-awareness of one's related strengths and weaknesses.

If the evolution of a conceptual self supports cultural niche seeking and an enhanced ability to use one's strengths in culturally important domains, then self-concepts should become differentiated during development and become stable and reflective of actual competencies before entering the world of adulthood. Academic self-concepts fit this pattern, as they become increasingly differentiated during schooling (Harter, 2006; Marsh & Shavelson, 1985) and are influenced by actual achievement (Valentine et al., 2004). Over time, a reciprocal relation between self-concepts and achievement in specific academic domains emerges, such that a more favorable earlier self-concept is associated with academic gains in that area (Wu et al., 2021). This pattern is consistent with the co-evolution of a conceptual self and cultural niche seeking, if we assume individuals differentially invest in refining their relative strengths, as they appear to in academic (Marsh & Martin, 2011) and nonacademic domains (Eccles & Wigfield, 2002; Marsh et al., 2006).

One important difference is that the benefits of culturally relevant self-concepts in traditional contexts are typically more concrete and immediate (e.g., hunting in hunter-gatherer societies) than the benefits of long-term investment in learning abstract academic knowledge. The latter appear to require more explicit cultural supports that foster their valuation than is likely to be needed in more traditional contexts. These would include supports in classroom settings (e.g., emphasizing inventors) and in family contexts. International differences in mathematics achievement, for instance, are related in part to cultural variation in how much these competencies are valued, which in turn influences the rigor of the curriculum and parental expectations for investment in this learning (Stevenson & Stigler, 1992). Relative to European Americans, the Asian-American advantage in academic achievement (including mathematics) is largely related to parental expectations and relative focus on academic achievement (Hsin & Xie, 2014), but these advantages decline over generations, in keeping with wider cultural valuation (or not) of academic competencies (Sakamoto et al., 2009).

## 5 Instruction Implications and Research

The likely contributions of the default mode network to mathematical and other discoveries and innovations seems to support the use of discovery learning as an instructional approach (Gray, 2016). The approach might work for some areas of mathematics, as an example, if the implicit (e.g., organization of supporting brain systems) structure of relevant folk abilities, such as the ANS, object processing, and navigation systems, had a one-to-one correspondence with the associated mathematical concepts and if engaging these systems resulted in an *explicit* understanding of this structure. For instance, the navigation system provides an *implicit* understanding that the fastest way to get from one place to another is to go "as the crow flies," and this was made explicit in a formal Euclidean postulate (West et al., 1982, p. 221): "a line can be drawn from any point to any point (In Euclidean geometry, a line is a straight line)." However, navigation does not result in an explicit understanding of the mathematical definition of a line; this has to be taught. More generally, Hadamard's (1945) descriptions of the processes underlying actual mathematical discoveries indicate that these often require continual focus and effort over long periods of time, a conceptual representation of the desired goal to be solved, and considerable background knowledge. These conditions cannot be replicated in classrooms with students who are essentially mathematical novices, and novices in all other secondary domains.

The most fundamental educational implication stems from the differences in the brain and cognitive networks and behavioral biases that support the development of primary and secondary abilities. Many of the scaffolds for the former emerge during prenatal and early postnatal development, and the full abilities emerge without instruction or much cognitive effort, as long as children engage in species-typical activities. Many of these brain and behavioral scaffolds have a deep evolutionary history and are evident in one form or another across species (e.g., E. A. Murray et al., 2018). We do not have this deep evolutionary history for academic domains and thus the same types of built-in scaffolds are neither expected nor found, as was described for reading and aspects of mathematics. As a result, the built-in structure that guides the development of primary folk abilities, such as language, needs to be provided by instructional materials, teaching practices, and cultural valuation for secondary abilities, such as reading and writing.

Moreover, the knowledge embedded in primary abilities is implicit: the reading of facial expressions or navigating from one place to another does not need to be explicitly understood to achieve these ends, because the underlying brain networks guide the associated behaviors and cognitions (Geary, 1995). Secondary knowledge and abilities, such as reading fluency, can become automatic and implicit but not without considerable practice (Cooper & Sweller, 1987; Kirschner et al., 2006; Winegard et al., 2018b). Before this point, instruction needs to provide an explicit structure to the knowledge to be learned, as exemplified by worked examples or step-by-step examples of how to solve one type of problem or another (Sweller & Cooper, 1985). The degree of needed external structure will vary from one student to the next based on the earlier described factors that influence educational outcomes, including cognitive ability, conscientiousness, and academic self-concepts and anxiety, as well as prior knowledge in the domain (Cronbach & Snow, 1977; Geary, 2007; Mayer, 2004; Schneider & Preckel, 2017; Sweller et al., 2019; Walberg, 1984).

The benefits of an organized, explicit curriculum were demonstrated with Project Follow Through (United States), which was the largest educational intervention ever conducted (Stebbins, 1977). The study provided a quasi-experimental evaluation of instructional approaches and included about 200,000 children across 180 communities. Each participating school partnered with a university or related group to develop and implement an intervention spanning four years from kindergarten through third grade grounded in differing principles and foci. These reflected basic teaching philosophy and broadly included direct instruction, cognitive approaches (e.g., focus on problem solving), and social/affective approaches focusing on, for instance, self-efficacy. The educational goals ranged from a focus on mastery of basic skills to more complex problem solving and conceptual understanding. Overall, children in the direct instruction programs with a focus on basic skills and mastery had better outcomes on basic skills, problem solving, and had a better academic self-concept than did students in the other programs. There was some fade-out over time, but many of these gains were maintained through the elementary school years (Meyer, 1984; Meyer et al., 1983).

The results were of course roundly criticized (House et al., 1978), but nonetheless consistent with an evolutionary perspective on learning and with findings from the evolutionarily informed cognitive load theory. The latter incorporates the working memory/attentional demands of instructional materials and approaches and students' prior knowledge in the domain into teaching strategies (Sweller et al., 2019). Other recent studies suggest that framing secondary concepts in primary scenarios (e.g., placing kin and nonkin in different groups to introduce mathematical sets) can improve students' engagement and motivation in secondary learning and sometimes improve learning itself (Alipour et al., 2023; Lespiau & Tricot, 2019, 2022a, 2022b).

Although much remains to be learned, there seems to be a consensus that unassisted, student-driven discovery learning is less effective than direct instruction (Alfieri et al., 2011; Zhang et al., 2022), but for some academic content, instructional approaches that include a combination of direct instruction and guided discovery are sometimes more effective than direct instruction alone (Alfieri et al., 2011; de Jong et al., 2023). Guided instruction where the teacher and instructional materials provide some structure to learning is consistent with an evolutionary perspective because it organizes the students' learning episode in ways that would not occur with unguided discovery learning. The effective use of this approach, however, is dependent on factors emphasized in cognitive load theory, including a firm understanding of basic knowledge in the area, which is best learned through direct instruction, and the attentional demands of the learning episode.

## 6 Conclusion

Modern education is an unprecedented social intervention designed to prepare students for life in evolutionarily novel WEIRD societies. The goal is to coax the brain into processing information and understand concepts that it did not evolve to process or understand, as well as to organize children's activities so that these goals are met. The long-standing debates regarding educational practices, especially child-centered unguided discovery learning methods and other romantic views, as contrasted with more direct, explicit, and teacher directed learning can be put to bed from an evolutionary perspective. This does not mean there is no place for guided (teacher aided) discovery learning or that all instruction needs to be direct and explicit. As noted, the most effective approach will depend on the secondary content and students' prior knowledge. The point is that the basic premises of discovery learning, constructivism, and related approaches are well suited for the developmental elaboration of primary abilities, but this is only because their acquisition is aided by built-in brain, cognitive, and motivational scaffolds that support this learning.

These scaffolds exist because primary abilities have a deep evolutionary history, as contrasted with a shallow cultural history for secondary abilities. To be sure, there has likely been some evolutionary section for secondary learning, but it is neither deep nor universal, and thus the child-driven behaviors that elaborate primary abilities are mismatched with the activities that promote secondary learning. This evolutionary framing helps us to understand why language learning is easier than learning to read; why children are more interested in socializing than learning mathematics; and, why their self-concepts are more centered on physical and social traits than on the secondary abilities that will make them successful as an adult in WEIRD societies. The approach also highlights the importance of an explicit, goal-directed curriculum and explicit instructional approaches that provide the same types of structure to students' secondary learning that is provided by the inherent scaffolds that support the developmental fleshing out of primary abilities.

# References

Abrams, D., & Hogg, M. A. (Eds.) (1990). *Social identity theory: Constructive and critical advances*. Springer-Verlag.

Adolphs, R. (1999). Social cognition and the human brain. *Trends in Cognitive Sciences*, *3*(12), 469–479. https://doi.org/10.1016/S1364-6613(99)01399-6.

Alexander, R. D. (1989). Evolution of the human psyche. In P. Mellars, & C. Stringer (Eds.), *The human revolution: Behavioural and biological perspectives on the origins of modern humans* (pp. 455–513). Princeton University Press.

Alexander-Bloch, A., Giedd, J. N., & Bullmore, E. (2013). Imaging structural co-variance between human brain regions. *Nature Reviews Neuroscience*, *14* (5), 322–336. https://doi.org/10.1038/nrn3465.

Alfieri, L., Brooks, P. J., Aldrich, N. J., & Tenenbaum, H. R. (2011). Does discovery-based instruction enhance learning? *Journal of Educational Psychology*, *103*(1), 1–18. https://doi.org/10.1037/a0021017.

Alipour, M., Aminifar, E., Geary, D. C., & Ebrahimpour, R. (2023). Framing mathematical content in evolutionarily salient contexts improves students' learning motivation. *Learning and Motivation*, *82*, 101894. https://doi.org/10.1016/j.lmot.2023.101894.

Amalric, M., & Dehaene, S. (2018). Cortical circuits for mathematical knowledge: Evidence for a major subdivision within the brain's semantic networks. *Philosophical Transactions of the Royal Society B: Biological Sciences*, *373*(1740), 20160515. https://doi.org/10.1098/rstb.2016.0515.

Andrews-Hanna, J. R., Irving, Z. C., Fox, K. C. R., Spreng, R. N., & Christoff, K. (2017). The neuroscience of spontaneous thought: An evolving, interdisciplinary field. In F. Kieran, & C. Kieran (Eds.), *Oxford handbook of spontaneous thought and creativity* (pp. 1–47). Oxford University Press.

Andrews-Hanna, J. R., Smallwood, J., & Spreng, R. N. (2014). The default network and self- generated thought: Component processes, dynamic control, and clinical relevance. *Annals of the New York Academy of Sciences*, *1316*(1), 29–52. https://doi.org/10.1111/nyas.12360.

Anglim, J., Dunlop, P. D., Wee, S. et al. (2022). Personality and intelligence: A meta-analysis. *Psychological Bulletin*, *148*(5–6), 301–336. https://doi.org/10.1037/bul0000373.

Arnatkeviciute, A., Fulcher, B. D., Oldham, S. et al. (2021). Genetic influences on hub connectivity of the human connectome. *Nature Communications*, *12* (1), 4237. https://doi.org/10.1038/s41467-021-24306-2.

Ashcraft, M. H. (2002). Math anxiety: Personal, educational, and cognitive consequences. *Current Directions in Psychological Science, 11*(5), 181–185. https://doi.org/10.1111/1467-8721.00196.

Ashcraft, M. H., & Krause, J. A. (2007). Working memory, math performance, and math anxiety. *Psychonomic Bulletin & Review, 14*(2), 243–248. https://doi.org/10.3758/BF03194059.

Assaf, Y., Bouznach, A., Zomet, O., Marom, A., & Yovel, Y. (2020). Conservation of brain connectivity and wiring across the mammalian class. *Nature Neuroscience, 23*(7), 805–808. https://doi.org/10.1038/s41593-020-0641-7.

Atit, K., Power, J. R., Pigott, T. et al. (2022).Examining the relations between spatial skills and mathematical performance: A meta-analysis. *Psychonomic Bulletin & Review, 29*, 699–720. https://doi.org/10.3758/s13423-021-02012-w.

Atran, S. (1998). Folk biology and the anthropology of science: Cognitive universals and cultural particulars. *Behavioral and Brain Sciences, 21*(4), 547–609. https://doi.org/10.1017/S0140525X98001277.

Baddeley, A., Gathercole, S., & Papagno, C. (1998). The phonological loop as a language learning device. *Psychological Review, 105*(1), 158–173. https://doi.org/10.1037/0033-295X.105.1.158.

Bae, C. J., Douka, K., & Petraglia, M. D. (2017). On the origin of modern humans: Asian perspectives. *Science, 358*(6368), eaai9067. https://doi.org/10.1126/science.aai9067.

Bailey, D. H., & Geary, D. C. (2009). Hominid brain evolution: Testing climatic, ecological, and social competition models. *Human Nature, 20*(1), 67–79. https://doi.org/10.1007/s12110-008-9054-0.

Baloglu, M., & Koçak, R. (2006). A multivariate investigation of the differences in mathematics anxiety. *Personality and Individual Differences, 40*(7), 1325–1335. https://doi.org/10.1016/j.paid.2005.10.009.

Bandura, A. (2001). Social cognitive theory: An agentic perspective. *Annual Review of Psychology, 52*, 1–26. https://doi.org/10.1146/annurev.psych.52.1.1.

Barbey, A. K. (2018). Network neuroscience theory of human intelligence. *Trends in Cognitive Sciences, 22*(1), 8–20. https://doi.org/10.1016/j.tics.2017.10.001.

Barkow, J. H. (1975). Prestige and culture: A biosocial interpretation. *Current Anthropology, 16*, 553–572. www.jstor.org/stable/2741630.

Barks, S. K., Parr, L. A., & Rilling, J. K. (2015). The default mode network in chimpanzees (*Pan troglodytes*) is similar to that of humans. *Cerebral Cortex, 25*(2), 538–544. https://doi.org/10.1093/cercor/bht253.

Barth, H. C., & Paladino, A. M. (2011). The development of numerical estimation: Evidence against a representational shift. *Developmental Science, 14*, 125–135. https://doi.org/10.1111/j.1467-7687.2010.00962.x.

Barton, R. A., & Dean, P. (1993). Comparative evidence indicating neural specialization for predatory behaviour in mammals. *Proceedings of the Royal Society of London B: Biological Sciences*, *254*(1339), 63–68. https://doi.org/10.1098/rspb.1993.0127.

Bassett, D. S., Wymbs, N. F., Porter, M. A. et al. (2011). Dynamic reconfiguration of human brain networks during learning. *Proceedings of the National Academy of Sciences of the United States of America*, *108*(18), 7641–7646. https://doi.org/10.1073/pnas.1018985108.

Basten, U., Hilger, K., & Fiebach, C. J. (2015). Where smart brains are different: A quantitative meta-analysis of functional and structural brain imaging studies on intelligence. *Intelligence*, *51*, 10–27. https://doi.org/10.1016/j.intell.2015.04.009.

Beaty, R. E., Benedek, M., Barry Kaufman, S., & Silvia, P. J. (2015). Default and executive network coupling supports creative idea production. *Scientific Reports*, *5*(1), 10964. https://doi.org/10.1038/srep10964.

Bennett, S. H., Kirby, A. J., & Finnerty, G. T. (2018). Rewiring the connectome: Evidence and effects. *Neuroscience & Biobehavioral Reviews*, *88*, 51–62. https://doi.org/10.1016/j.neubiorev.2018.03.001.

Beran, M. J., Menzel, C. R., Parrish, A. E. et al. (2016). Primate cognition: Attention, episodic memory, prospective memory, self-control, and metacognition as examples of cognitive control in nonhuman primates. *Wiley Interdisciplinary Reviews: Cognitive Science*, *7*(5), 294–316. https://doi.org/10.1002/wcs.1397.

Berlin, B., Breedlove, D. E., & Raven, P. H. (1966). Folk taxonomies and biological classification. *Science*, *154*(3746), 273–275. https://doi.org/10.1126/science.154.3746.27.

Berlin, B., Breedlove, D. E., & Raven, P. H. (1973). General principles of classification and nomenclature in folk biology. *American Anthropologist*, *75*(1), 214–242. https://doi.org/10.1525/aa.1973.75.1.02a00140.

Bernieri, F. J., Reznick, J. S., & Rosenthal, R. (1988). Synchrony, pseudosynchrony, and dissynchrony: Measuring the entrainment process in mother-infant interactions. *Journal of Personality and Social Psychology*, *54*, 243–253. https://doi.org/10.1037/0022-3514.54.2.243.

Betzel, R. F., Gu, S., Medaglia, J. D., Pasqualetti, F., & Bassett, D. S. (2016). Optimally controlling the human connectome: The role of network topology. *Scientific Reports*, *6*(1), 30770. https://doi.org/10.1038/srep30770.

Bhaduri, A., Sandoval-Espinosa, C., Otero-Garcia, M. et al. (2021). An atlas of cortical arealization identifies dynamic molecular signatures. *Nature*, *598*(7879), 200–204. https://doi.org/10.1038/s41586-021-03910-8.

Bi, X., Zhou, L., Zhang, J. J. et al. (2023). Lineage-specific accelerated sequences underlying primate evolution. *Science Advances*, *9*(22), eadc9507. https://doi.org/10.1126/sciadv.adc9507.

Bjorklund, D. F. (2018). How children invented humanity. *Child Development*, *89*(5), 1462–1466. https://doi.org/10.1111/cdev.13020.

Bjorklund, D. F., & Pellegrini, A. D. (2002). *The origins of human nature: Evolutionary developmental psychology.* American Psychological Association.

Bonfanti, L., & Charvet, C. J. (2021). Brain plasticity in humans and model systems: Advances, challenges, and future directions. *International Journal of Molecular Sciences*, *22*(17), 9358. https://doi.org/10.3390/ijms22179358.

Botvinick, M. M., Braver, T. S., Barch, D. M., Carter, C. S., & Cohen, J. D. (2001). Conflict monitoring and cognitive control. *Psychological Review*, *108*(3), 624–652. https://doi.org/10.1037/0033-295X.108.3.624.

Bouhali, F., de Schotten, M. T., Pinel, P. et al. (2014). Anatomical connections of the visual word form area. *Journal of Neuroscience*, *34*(46), 15402–15414. https://doi.org/10.1523/JNEUROSCI.4918-13.2014.

Bradley, L., & Bryant, P. E. (1983). Categorizing sounds and learning to read – a causal connection. *Nature*, *301*(5899), 419–421. https://doi.org/10.1038/301419a0.

Brem, S., Maurer, U., Kronbichler, M. et al. (2020). Visual word form processing deficits driven by severity of reading impairments in children with developmental dyslexia. *Scientific Reports*, *10*(1), 18728. https://doi.org/10.1038/s41598-020-75111-8.

Brodmann, K. (1909). *Vergleichende Lokalisationslehre der Grosshirnrinde in ihren Prinzipien dargestellt auf Grund des Zellenbaues.* [Comparative localization of the cerebral cortex based on cell composition.] Barth.

Broglio, C., Martín-Monzón, I., Ocaña, F. M. et al. (2015). Hippocampal pallium and map-like memories through vertebrate evolution. *Journal of Behavioral and Brain Science*, *5*(3), 54939. https://doi.org/10.4236/jbbs.2015.53011.

Brothers, L., & Ring, B. (1992). A neuroethological framework for the representation of minds. *Journal of Cognitive Neuroscience*, *4*(2), 107–118. https://doi.org/10.1162/jocn.1992.4.2.107.

Brown, R. (1973). *A first language: The early stages.* Harvard University Press. https://doi.org/10.4159/harvard.9780674732469.

Buckner, R. L., & DiNicola, L. M. (2019). The brain's default network: Updated anatomy, physiology and evolving insights. *Nature Reviews Neuroscience*, *20*(10), 593–608. https://doi.org/10.1038/s41583-019-0212-7.

Bugental, D. B. (2000). Acquisition of the algorithms of social life: A domain-based approach. *Psychological Bulletin, 126*(2), 187–219. https://doi.org/10.1037/0033-2909.126.2.187.

Burgos-Robles, A., Gothard, K. M., Monfils, M. H., Morozov, A., & Vicentic, A. (2019). Conserved features of anterior cingulate networks support observational learning across species. *Neuroscience & Biobehavioral Reviews, 107*, 215–228. https://doi.org/10.1016/j.neubiorev.2019.09.009.

Burgoyne, A. P., & Engle, R. W. (2020). Attention control: A cornerstone of higher-order cognition. *Current Directions in Psychological Science, 29*(6), 624–630. https://doi.org/10.1177/0963721420969371.

Cadwell, C. R., Bhaduri, A., Mostajo-Radji, M. A., Keefe, M. G., & Nowakowski, T. J. (2019). Development and arealization of the cerebral cortex. *Neuron, 103*(6), 980–1004. https://doi.org/10.1016/j.neuron.2019.07.009.

Caporael, L. R. (1997). The evolution of truly social cognition: The core configurations model. *Personality & Social Psychology Review, 1*(4), 276–298. https://doi.org/10.1207/s15327957pspr0104_1.

Carey, S. (2009). *The origin of concepts*. Oxford University Press.

Carroll, J. B. (1993). *Human cognitive abilities: A survey of factor-analytic studies*. Cambridge University Press.

Casey, B. M., & Ganley, C. M. (2021). An examination of gender differences in spatial skills and math attitudes in relation to mathematics success: A bio-psycho-social model. *Developmental Review, 60*, 100963. https://doi.org/10.1016/j.dr.2021.100963.

Castaldi, E., Vignaud, A., & Eger, E. (2020). Mapping subcomponents of numerical cognition in relation to functional and anatomical landmarks of human parietal cortex. *Neuroimage, 221*, 117210. https://doi.org/10.1016/j.neuroimage.2020.117210.

Cattell, R. B. (1963). Theory of fluid and crystallized intelligence: A critical experiment. *Journal of Educational Psychology, 54*(1), 1–22. https://doi.org/10.1037/h0046743.

Cavanna, A. E., & Trimble, M. R. (2006). The precuneus: A review of its functional anatomy and behavioural correlates. *Brain, 129*(3), 564–583. https://doi.org/10.1093/brain/awl004.

Caviola, S., Toffalini, E., Giofrè, D. et al. (2022). Math performance and academic anxiety forms, from sociodemographic to cognitive aspects: A meta-analysis on 906,311 participants. *Educational Psychology Review, 34*(1), 363–399. https://doi.org/10.1007/s10648-021-09618-5.

Chen, L., Wassermann, D., Abrams, D. A. et al. (2019). The visual word form area (VWFA) is part of both language and attention circuitry. *Nature Communications, 10*(1), 5601. https://doi.org/10.1038/s41467-019-13634-z.

Cheung, P., Rubenson, M., & Barner, D. (2017). To infinity and beyond: Children generalize the successor function to all possible numbers years after learning to count. *Cognitive Psychology, 92*, 22–36. http://doi.org/10.1016/j.cogpsych.2016.11.002.

Christov-Moore, L., Simpson, E. A., Coudé, G. et al. (2014). Empathy: Gender effects in brain and behavior. *Neuroscience & Biobehavioral Reviews, 46*(4), 604–627. https://doi.org/10.1016/j.neubiorev.2014.09.001.

Clark, G. (2008). *A farewell to alms: A brief economic history of the world*. Princeton University Press.

Clark, G. (2016). Microbes and markets: Was the Black Death an economic revolution? *Journal of Demographic Economics, 82*(2), 139–165. https://doi.org/10.1017/dem.2016.6.

Clement, J. (1982). Students' preconceptions in introductory mechanics. *American Journal of Physics, 50*(1), 66–71. https://doi.org/10.1119/1.12989.

Cohen, D. J., & Blanc-Goldhammer, D. (2011). Numerical bias in bounded and unbounded number line tasks. *Psychonomic Bulletin & Review, 18*, 331–338. https://doi.org/10.3758/s13423-011-0059-z.

Cohen Kadosh, R., Bahrami, B., Walsh, V. et al. (2011). Specialization in the human brain: The case of numbers. *Frontiers in Human Neuroscience, 5*, 62. https://doi.org/10.3389/fnhum.2011.00062.

Cooper, G., & Sweller, J. (1987). Effects of schema acquisition and rule automation on mathematical problem-solving transfer. *Journal of Educational Psychology, 79*(4), 347–362. https://doi.org/10.1037/0022-0663.79.4.347.

Costantini, G., & Perugini, M. (2016). The network of conscientiousness. *Journal of Research in Personality, 65*, 68–88. https://doi.org/10.1016/j.jrp.2016.10.003.

Coste, C. P., & Kleinschmidt, A. (2016). Cingulo-opercular network activity maintains alertness. *Neuroimage, 128*, 264–272. https://doi.org/10.1016/j.neuroimage.2016.01.026.

Cowan, N. (1998). *Attention and memory: An integrated framework*. Oxford University Press.

Cox, C., Bergmann, C., Fowler, E. et al. (2023). A systematic review and Bayesian meta-analysis of the acoustic features of infant-directed speech. *Nature Human Behaviour, 7*(1), 114–133. https://doi.org/10.1038/s41562-022-01452-1.

Cronbach, L. J., & Snow, R. E. (1977). *Aptitudes and instructional methods: A handbook for research on interactions*. Irvington.

Csikszentmihalyi, M., & Hunter, J. (2003). Happiness in everyday life: The uses of experience sampling. *Journal of Happiness Studies, 4*, 185–199. https://doi.org/10.1023/A:1024409732742.

Currie, T. E., Turchin, P., Turner, E., & Gavrilets, S. (2020). Duration of agriculture and distance from the steppe predict the evolution of large-scale human societies in Afro-Eurasia. *Humanities and Social Sciences Communications*, *7*(1), 1–8. https://doi.org/10.1057/s41599-020-0516-2.

Dantzig, T. (1930). *Number: The language of science*. Macmillan.

Darwin, C., & Wallace A. (1858). On the tendency of species to form varieties, and on the perpetuation of varieties and species by natural means of selection. *Journal of the Linnean Society of London, Zoology*, *3*(9), 45–62. https://doi.org/10.1111/j.1096-3642.1858.tb02500.x.

Davey, C. G., Pujol, J., & Harrison, B. J. (2016). Mapping the self in the brain's default mode network. *NeuroImage*, *132*, 390–397. https://doi.org/10.1016/j.neuroimage.2016.02.022.

Davis, C. P., & Yee, E. (2019). Features, labels, space, and time: Factors supporting taxonomic relationships in the anterior temporal lobe and thematic relationships in the angular gyrus. *Language, Cognition and Neuroscience*, *34*(10), 1347–1357. https://doi.org/10.1080/23273798.2018.1479530.

De Dreu, C., Nijstad, B. A., & Baas, M. (2023). Human creativity: Functions, mechanisms and social conditioning. *Advances in Experimental Social Psychology*.

de Jong, T., Lazonder, A. W., Chinn, C. A. et al. (2023). Let's talk evidence–The case for combining inquiry-based and direct instruction. *Educational Research Review*, *39*, 100536. https://doi:10.1016/j.edurev.2023.100536.

Dean, L. G., Vale, G. L., Laland, K. N., Flynn, E., & Kendal, R. L. (2014). Human cumulative culture: A comparative perspective. *Biological Reviews*, *89*(2), 284–301. https://doi.org/10.1111/brv.12053.

DeCasien, A. R., & Higham, J. P. (2019). Primate mosaic brain evolution reflects selection on sensory and cognitive specialization. *Nature Ecology & Evolution*, *3*(10), 1483–1493. https://doi.org/10.1038/s41559-019-0969-0.

DeCasien, A. R., Barton, R. A., & Higham, J. P. (2022). Understanding the human brain: insights from comparative biology. *Trends in Cognitive Sciences*, *26*(5), 432–445.https://doi.org/10.1016/j.tics.2022.02.003.

Dehaene, S., & Cohen, L. (2007). Cultural recycling of cortical maps. *Neuron*, *56*(2), 384–398. https://doi.org/10.1016/j.neuron.2007.10.004.

Dehaene, S., Izard, V., Spelke, E., & Pica, P. (2008). Log or linear? Distinct intuitions of the number scale in Western and Amazonian indigene cultures. *Science*, *320*, 1217–1220. https://doi.org/10.1126/science.1156540.

Dehaene, S., Pegado, F., Braga, L. W. et al. (2010). How learning to read changes the cortical networks for vision and language. *Science*, *330*(6009), 1359–1364. https://doi.org/10.1126/science.1194140.

Dehaene, S., Piazza, M., Pinel, P., & Cohen, L. (2003). Three parietal circuits for number processing. *Cognitive Neuropsychology*, *20*(3–6), 487–506. https://doi.org/10.1080/02643290244000239.

Dehaene-Lambertz, G., Montavont, A., Jobert, A. et al. (2010). Language or music, mother or Mozart? Structural and environmental influences on infants' language networks. *Brain and Language*, *114*(2), 53–65. https://doi.org/10.1016/j.bandl.2009.09.003.

Demetriou, A., Spanoudis, G., Shayer, M. et al. (2014). Relations between speed, working memory, and intelligence from preschool to adulthood: Structural equation modeling of 14 studies. *Intelligence*, *46*, 107–121. https://doi.org/10.1016/j.intell.2014.05.013.

Derex, M. (2022). Human cumulative culture and the exploitation of natural phenomena. *Philosophical Transactions of the Royal Society B*, *377*(1843), 20200311. https://doi.org/10.1098/rstb.2020.0311.

Dillon, M. R., Huang, Y., & Spelke, E. S. (2013). Core foundations of abstract geometry. *Proceedings of the National Academy of Sciences of the United States of America*, *110*, 14191–14195. https://doi.org/10.1073/pnas.1312640110.

Dotan, D., & Dehaene, S. (2016). On the origins of logarithmic number-to-position mapping. *Psychological Review*, *123*, 637–666. https://doi.org/10.1037/rev0000038.

Dowker, A., Sarkar, A., & Looi, C. Y. (2016). Mathematics anxiety: What have we learned in 60 years? *Frontiers in Psychology*, *7*, 508. https://doi.org/10.3389/fpsyg.2016.00508.

Dukas, R. (Ed.) (1998). *Cognitive ecology: The evolutionary ecology of information processing and decision making*. University of Chicago Press.

Dunbar, R. I. (1998). The social brain hypothesis. *Evolutionary Anthropology*, *6*(5), 178–190.https://doi.org/10.1002/(SICI)1520-6505(1998)6:5<178::AID-EVAN5>3.0.CO;2-8.

Dunbar, R. I. M. (1993). Coevolution of neocortical size, group size and language in humans. *Behavioral and Brain Sciences*, *16*(4), 681–735. https://doi.org/10.1017/S0140525X00032325.

Durkee, P. K., Lukaszewski, A. W., & Buss, D. M. (2019). Pride and shame: Key components of a culturally universal status management system. *Evolution and Human Behavior*, *40*, 470–478. https://doi.org/10.1016/j.evolhumbehav.2019.06.004.

Eagly, A. H. (1987). *Sex differences in social behavior: A social-role interpretation*. Erlbaum.

Eccles, J. S., & Wigfield, A. (2002). Motivational beliefs, values, and goals. *Annual Review of Psychology*, *53*, 109–132. https://doi.org/10.1146/annurev.psych.53.100901.135153.

Elton, S., Bishop, L. C., & Wood, B. (2001). Comparative context of Plio-Pleistocene hominin brain evolution. *Journal of Human Evolution, 41*(1), 1–27. https://doi.org/10.1006/jhev.2001.0475.

Engle, R. W., Kane, M. J., & Tuholski, S. W. (1999). Individual differences in working memory capacity and what they tell us about controlled attention, general fluid intelligence, and functions of the prefrontal cortex. In A. Miyake, & P. Shah (Eds.), *Models of working memory: Mechanisms of active maintenance and executive control* (pp. 102–134). Cambridge University Press.

Eskelson, T. C. (2020). How and why formal education originated in the emergence of civilization. *Journal of Education and Learning, 9*(2), 29–47. https://doi.org/10.5539/jel.v9n2p29.

Esnaola, I., Sesé, A., Antonio-Agirre, I., & Azpiazu, L. (2020). The development of multiple self-concept dimensions during adolescence. *Journal of Research on Adolescence, 30*, 100–114. https://doi.org/10.1111/jora.12451.

Fanta, V., Šálek, M., Zouhar, J., Sklenicka, P., & Storch, D. (2018). Equilibrium dynamics of European pre-industrial populations: The evidence of carrying capacity in human agricultural societies. *Proceedings of the Royal Society B: Biological Sciences, 285*(1871), 20172500. https://doi.org/10.1098/rspb.2017.2500.

Faust, T. E., Gunner, G., & Schafer, D. P. (2021). Mechanisms governing activity-dependent synaptic pruning in the developing mammalian CNS. *Nature Reviews Neuroscience, 22*(11), 657–673. https://doi.org/10.1038/s41583-021-00507-y.

Fedorenko, E., & Blank, I. A. (2020). Broca's area is not a natural kind. *Trends in Cognitive Sciences, 24*(4), 270–284. https://doi.org/10.1016/j.tics.2020.01.001.

Feigenson, L. , Dehaene, S., & Spelke, E. (2004). Core systems of number. *Trends in Cognitive Sciences, 8*(7), 307–314. https://doi.org/10.1016/j.tics.2004.05.002.

Feigenson, L., Libertus, M. E., & Halberda, J. (2013). Links between the intuitive sense of number and formal mathematics ability. *Child Development Perspectives, 7*, 74–79. http://dx.doi.org/10.1111/cdep.12019.

Fiske, S. T., & Taylor, S. E. (1991). *Social cognition* (2nd ed.). McGraw-Hill.

Flinn, M. V., Geary, D. C., & Ward, C. V. (2005). Ecological dominance, social competition, and coalitionary arms races: Why humans evolved extraordinary intelligence. *Evolution and Human Behavior, 26*(1), 10–46. https://doi.org/10.1016/j.evolhumbehav.2004.08.005.

Frey, S. H. (2008). Tool use, communicative gesture and cerebral asymmetries in the modern human brain. *Philosophical Transactions of the Royal Society B: Biological Sciences, 363*(1499), 1951–1957. https://doi.org/10.1098/rstb.2008.0008.

Gallistel, C. R. (1990). *The organization of learning*. The MIT Press.

Gallistel, C. R., & Gelman, R. (2000). Non-verbal numerical cognition: From reals to integers. *Trends in Cognitive Sciences, 4*(2), 59–65. https://doi.org/10.1016/s1364-6613(99)01424-2.

Gallup Jr, G. G. (1998). Self-awareness and the evolution of social intelligence. *Behavioural Processes, 42*, 239–247. https://doi.org/10.1016/S0376-6357 (97)00079-X.

Galor, O., & Klemp, M. (2019). Human genealogy reveals a selective advantage to moderate fecundity. *Nature Ecology & Evolution, 3*(5), 853–857. https://doi.org/10.1038/s41559-019-0846-x.

Gangopadhyay, P., Chawla, M., Dal Monte, O., & Chang, S. W. (2021). Prefrontal–amygdala circuits in social decision-making. *Nature Neuroscience, 24*(1), 5–18. https://doi.org/10.1038/s41593-020-00738-9.

Garin, C. M., Hori, Y., Everling, S. et al. (2022). An evolutionary gap in primate default mode network organization. *Cell Reports, 39*(2), 110669. https://doi.org/10.1016/j.celrep.2022.110669.

Geary, D. C. (1995). Reflections of evolution and culture in children's cognition: Implications for mathematical development and instruction. *American Psychologist, 50*(1), 24–37. https://doi.org/10.1037/0003-066X.50.1.24.

Geary, D. C. (2002). Principles of evolutionary educational psychology. *Learning and Individual Differences, 12*(4), 317–345. https://doi.org/10.1016/S1041-6080(02)00046-8.

Geary, D. C. (2005). *The origin of mind: Evolution of brain, cognition, and general intelligence*. American Psychological Association. https://doi.org/10.1037/10871-000.

Geary, D. C. (2007). Educating the evolved mind: Conceptual foundations for an evolutionary educational psychology. In J. S. Carlson, & J. R. Levin (Eds.), *Educating the evolved mind* (pp. 1–99, 177–202, Vol. 2, Psychological perspectives on contemporary educational issues). Information Age.

Geary, D. C. (2008). An evolutionarily informed education science. *Educational Psychologist, 43*(4), 279–295. https://doi.org/10.1080/00461520802392133.

Geary, D. C. (2018). Efficiency of mitochondrial functioning as the fundamental biological mechanism of general intelligence (*g*). *Psychological Review, 125*(6), 1028–1050. https://doi.org/10.1037/rev0000124.

Geary, D. C. (2020). Mitochondrial functions, cognition, and the evolution of intelligence: Reply to commentaries and moving forward. *Journal of Intelligence, 8*(4), 42. https://doi.org//10.3390/jintelligence8040042.

Geary, D. C. (2021). *Male, female: The evolution of human sex differences* (3rd ed.). American Psychological Association.

Geary, D. C. (2022). Sex, brain, and mathematics: An evolutionary perspective. *Developmental Review, 63*(1), 101010. https://doi.org/10.1016/j.dr.2021.101010.

Geary, D. C., & Berch, D. B. (2016). Evolution and children's cognitive and academic development. In D. C. Geary, & D. B. Berch (Eds.), *Evolutionary perspectives on child development and education* (pp. 217–249). Springer.

Geary, D. C., & Bjorklund, D. F. (2000). Evolutionary developmental psychology. *Child Development, 71*(1), 57–65. https://doi.org/10.1111/1467-8624.00118.

Geary, D. C. & Huffman, K. J. (2002). Brain and cognitive evolution: Forms of modularity and functions of mind. *Psychological Bulletin, 128*(5), 667–698. https://doi.org/10.1037/0033-2909.128.5.667.

Geary, D. C., & vanMarle, K. (2016). Young children's core symbolic and non-symbolic quantitative knowledge in the prediction of later mathematics achievement. *Developmental Psychology, 52*, 2130–2144. http://doi.org/10.1037/dev0000214.

Geary, D. C., & Xu, K. M. (2022). Evolution of self-awareness and the cultural emergence of academic and non-academic self-concepts. *Educational Psychology Review, 34*(4), 2323–2349. https://doi.org/10.1007/s10648-022-09669-2.

Geary, D. C., Berch, D. B., & Mann Koepke, K. (Eds.) (2015). *Evolutionary origins and early development of number processing.* Elsevier Academic Press.

Geary, D. C., Scofield, J. E., Hoard, M. K., & Nugent, L. (2021). Boys' advantage on the fractions number line is mediated by visuospatial attention: Evidence for a parietal-spatial contribution to number line learning. *Developmental Science, 24*, e13063. https://doi.org//10.1111/desc.13063.

Geary, D. C., Hoard, M. K., Nugent, L., & Ünal, Z. E. (2023). Sex differences in developmental pathways to mathematical competence. *Journal of Educational Psychology, 115*, 212–228. https://doi.org/10.1037/edu0000763.

Geary, D. C., Hoard, M. K., Nugent, L., Ünal, Z. E., & Greene, N. R. (2023). Sex differences and similarities in relations between mathematics achievement, attitudes, and anxiety: A 7th-to-9th grade longitudinal study. *Journal of Educational Psychology, 115*(5), 767–782. http://dx.doi.org/10.1037/edu0000793.

Geary, D. C., vanMarle, K., Chu, F., Hoard, M. K., & Nugent, L. (2019). Predicting age of becoming a cardinal principle knower. *Journal of Educational Psychology, 111*(2), 256–267. https://doi.org/10.1037/edu0000277.

Gelman, R. (1990). First principles organize attention to and learning about relevant data: Number and animate-inanimate distinction as examples. *Cognitive Science, 14*(1), 79–106. https://doi.org/10.1207/s15516709cog1401_5.

Gelman, S. A. (2003). *The essential child: Origins of essentialism in everyday thought*. Oxford University Press. https://doi.org/10.1093/acprof:oso/9780195154061.001.0001.

Gernsbacher, M. A., & Kaschak, M. P. (2003). Neuroimaging studies of language production and comprehension. *Annual Review of Psychology, 54*, 91–114. https://doi.org//10.1146/annurev.psych.54.101601.145128.

Ghio, M., Cara, C., & Tettamanti, M. (2021). The prenatal brain readiness for speech processing: A review on foetal development of auditory and primordial language networks. *Neuroscience & Biobehavioral Reviews, 128*, 709–719. https://doi.org/10.1016/j.neubiorev.2021.07.009.

Goldin, C. (1999). *A brief history of education in the United States* (0898–2937). Cambridge, MA: National Bureau of Economic Research. www.nber.org/papers/h0119.

Gong, Y., Greenbaum, J., & Deng, H.-W. (2019). A statistical approach to fine-mapping for the identification of potential causal variants related to human intelligence. *Journal of Human Genetics, 64*, 781–787. https://doi.org/10.1038/s10038-019-0623-3.

Gopnik, A., & Wellman, H. M. (2012). Reconstructing constructivism: Causal models, Bayesian learning mechanisms, and the theory theory. *Psychological Bulletin, 138*(6), 1085–1108. https://doi.org/10.1037/a0028044.

Gotlieb, R. J., Hyde, E., Immordino-Yang, M. H., & Kaufman, S. B. (2019). Imagination is the seed of creativity. In J. C. Kaufman, & R. J. Sternberg (Eds.), *The Cambridge handbook of creativity* (2nd ed., pp. 709–731). Cambridge University Press.

Gould, S. J., & Vrba, E. S. (1982). Exaptation – a missing term in the science of form. *Paleobiology, 8*(1), 4–15. https://doi.org/10.1017/S0094837300004310.

Grasby, K. L., Jahanshad, N., Painter, J. N. et al. (2020). The genetic architecture of the human cerebral cortex. *Science, 367*(6484), eaay6690. https://doi.org/10.1126/science.aay6690.

Gray, P. (2016). Children's natural ways of educating themselves still work: Even for the three Rs. In D. C. Geary, & D. B. Berch (Eds.), *Evolutionary perspectives on child development and education* (pp. 67–93). Springer. https://doi.org/10.1007/978-3-319-29986-0_3.

Greenough, W. T. (1991). Experience as a component of normal development: Evolutionary considerations. *Developmental Psychology, 27*(1), 14–17. https://doi.org/10.1037/0012-1649.27.1.14.

Greenough, W. T., Black, J. E., & Wallace, C. S. (1987). Experience and brain development. *Child Development, 58*(3), 539–559. www.jstor.org/stable/1130197.

Hadamard, J. (1945). *The mathematician's mind: Psychology of invention in the mathematical field.* Dover.

Hagmann, P., Sporns, O., Madan, N. et al. (2010). White matter maturation reshapes structural connectivity in the late developing human brain. *Proceedings of the National Academy of Sciences of the United States of America, 107*(44), 19067–19072. https://doi.org/10.1073/pnas.1009073107.

Halberda, J., & Feigenson, L. (2008). Developmental change in the acuity of the "Number Sense": The approximate number system in 3-, 4-, 5-, and 6-year-olds and adults. *Developmental Psychology, 44*(5), 1457–1465. https://doi.org/10.1037/a0012682.

Hamilton, M. J., & Walker, R. S. (2018). A stochastic density-dependent model of long-term population dynamics in hunter-gatherer populations. *Evolutionary Ecology Research, 19*(1), 85–102. www.evolutionary-ecology.com/issues/v19/n01/iiar3085.pdf.

Hamilton, W. D. (1964). The genetical evolution of social behaviour. II. *Journal of Theoretical Biology, 7*(1), 17–52. https://doi.org/10.1016/0022-5193(64)90039-6.

Harter, S. (2006). The self. In N. Eisenberg, W. Damon, & R. M. Lerner (Eds.), *Handbook of child psychology: Social, emotional, and personality development* (pp. 505–570). John Wiley.

Hawes, Z., & Ansari, D. (2020). What explains the relationship between spatial and mathematical skills? A review of evidence from brain and behavior. *Psychonomic Bulletin & Review, 27*, 465–482. https://doi.org/10.3758/s13423-019-01694-7.

Hecht, E. E., Gutman, D. A., Bradley, B. A., Preuss, T. M., & Stout, D. (2015). Virtual dissection and comparative connectivity of the superior longitudinal fasciculus in chimpanzees and humans. *Neuroimage, 108*, 124–137. https://doi.org/10.1016/j.neuroimage.2014.12.039.

Hegarty, M. (2004). Mechanical reasoning by mental simulation. *Trends in Cognitive Sciences, 8*(6), 280–285. https://doi.org/10.1016/j.tics.2004.04.001.

Heinonen, J., Numminen, J., Hlushchuk, Y. et al. (2016). Default mode and executive networks areas: Association with the serial order in divergent thinking. *PLoS ONE, 11*(9), e0162234. https://doi.org/10.1371/journal.pone.0162234.

Hembree, R. (1990). The nature, effects, and relief of mathematics anxiety. *Journal for Research in Mathematics Education, 21*(1), 33–46. https://doi.org/10.2307/749455.

Henrich, J., Heine, S. J., & Norenzayan, A. (2010). The weirdest people in the world? *Behavioral and Brain Sciences, 33*(2–3), 61–135. https://doi.org/10.1017/S0140525X0999152X.

Herbet, G., & Duffau, H. (2020). Revisiting the functional anatomy of the human brain: Toward a meta-networking theory of cerebral functions. *Physiological Reviews*, *100*(3), 1181–1228. https://doi.org/10.1152/physrev.00033.2019.

Hermann, R., Dolfini, A., Crellin, R. J., Wang, Q., & Uckelmann, M. (2020). Bronze age swordsmanship: New insights from experiments and wear analysis. *Journal of Archaeological Method and Theory*, *27*(4), 1040–1083. https://doi.org/10.1007/s10816-020-09451-0.

Hewstone, M., Rubin, M., & Willis, H. (2002). Intergroup bias. *Annual Review of Psychology*, *53*, 575–604. https://doi.org/10.1146/annurev.psych.53.100901.135109.

Hirschfeld, K. (2015). *Gangster states: Organized crime, kleptocracy and political collapse*. Palgrave-MacMillan.

Horn, J. L., & Cattell, R. B. (1966). Refinement and test of the theory of fluid and crystallized general intelligence. *Journal of Educational Psychology*, *57* (5), 253–270. https://doi.org/10.1037/h0023816.

Horowitz, D. L. (2001). *The deadly ethnic riot*. University of California Press.

House, E., Glass, G., McLean, L., & Walker, D. (1978). No simple answer: Critique of the Follow through evaluation. *Harvard Educational Review*, *48*, 462–464. https://doi.org/10.17763/haer.48.2.j2167r4594027x87.

Howard-Jones, P. A., Jay, T., Mason, A., & Jones, H. (2016). Gamification of learning deactivates the default mode network. *Frontiers in Psychology*, *6*, 1891. https://doi.org/10.3389/fpsyg.2015.01891.

Hsin, A., & Xie, Y. (2014). Explaining Asian Americans' academic advantage over whites. *Proceedings of the National Academy of Sciences of the United America*, *111*, 8416–8421. https://doi.org/10.1073/pnas.1406402111.

Hubbard, E. M., Piazza, M., Pinel, P., & Dehaene, S. (2005). Interactions between number and space in parietal cortex. *Nature Reviews Neuroscience*, *6*, 435–448. https://doi.org/10.1038/nrn1684.

Huffman, K. J., Nelson, J., Clarey, J., & Krubitzer, L. (1999). Organization of somatosensory cortex in three species of marsupials, *Dasyurus hallucatus, Dactylopsila trivirgata*, and *Monodelphis domestica*: Neural correlates of morphological specializations. *Journal of Comparative Neurology*, *403*(1), 5–32. https://doi.org/10.1002/(SICI)1096-9861(19990105)403:1<5::AID-CNE2>3.0.CO;2-F.

Humphrey, N. K. (1976). The social function of intellect. In P. P. G. Bateson, & R. A. Hinde (Eds.), *Growing points in ethology* (pp. 303–317). Cambridge University Press.

Hunter, J. E., & Schmidt, F. L. (1996). Intelligence and job performance: Economic and social implications. *Psychology, Public Policy, and Law, 2* (3–4), 447–472. https://doi.org/10.1037/1076-8971.2.3-4.447.

Imuta, K., Henry, J. D., Slaughter, V., Selcuk, B., & Ruffman, T. (2016). Theory of mind and prosocial behavior in childhood: A meta-analytic review. *Developmental Psychology, 52*(8), 1192–1205. https://doi.org/10.1037/dev0000140.

Jensen, A. R., & Munro, E. (1979). Reaction time, movement time, and intelligence. *Intelligence, 3*(2), 121–126. https://doi.org/10.1016/0160-2896 (79)90010-2.

Jernigan, T. L., Baaré, W. F., Stiles, J., & Madsen, K. S. (2011). Postnatal brain development: Structural imaging of dynamic neurodevelopmental processes. *Progress in Brain Research, 189*, 77–92. https://doi.org/10.1016/B978-0-444-53884-0.00019-1.

Jitendra, A. K., & Woodward, J. (2019). The role of visual representations in mathematical word problems. In D. C. Geary, D. B. Berch, & K. Mann Koepke (Eds.), *Cognitive foundations for improving mathematical learning* (pp. 269–293). Elsevier Academic Press.

Johnson, M. H., Senju, A., & Tomalski, P. (2015). The two-process theory of face processing: Modifications based on two decades of data from infants and adults. *Neuroscience & Biobehavioral Reviews, 50*, 169–179. https://doi.org/10.1016/j.neubiorev.2014.10.009.

Johnson-Laird, P. N. (1983). *Mental models*. Cambridge University Press.

Jung, R. E., & Haier, R. J. (2007). The Parieto-Frontal Integration Theory (P-FIT) of intelligence: Converging neuroimaging evidence. *Behavioral and Brain Sciences, 30*(2), 135–154. https://doi.org/10.1017/S0140525X 07001185.

Kaas, J. H. (1982). The segregation of function in the nervous system: Why do the sensory systems have so many subdivisions? *Contributions to Sensory Physiology, 7*, 201–240. https://doi.org/10.1016/B978-0-12-151807-3.50012-4.

Kaiser, M. K., McCloskey, M., & Proffitt, D. R. (1986). Development of intuitive theories of motion: Curvilinear motion in the absence of external forces. *Developmental Psychology, 22*(1), 67–71. doi.org/10.1037/0012-1649.22.1.67.

Kanazawa, S. (2008). Temperature and evolutionary novelty as forces behind the evolution of general intelligence. *Intelligence, 36*(2), 99–108. https://doi.org/10.1016/j.intell.2007.04.001.

Kane, M. J., & Engle, R. W. (2002). The role of prefrontal cortex in work-ing-memory capacity, executive attention, and general fluid intelligence: An individual-differences perspective. *Psychonomic Bulletin & Review, 9*(4), 637–671. https://doi.org/10.3758/BF03196323.

Kaplan, H., Hill, K., Lancaster, J., & Hurtado, A. M. (2000). A theory of human life history evolution: Diet, intelligence, and longevity. *Evolutionary Anthropology, 9*(4), 156–185. https://doi.org/10.1002/1520-6505(2000) 9:4<156::AID-EVAN5>3.0.CO;2-7.

Kell, H. J., Lubinski, D., Benbow, C. P., & Steiger, J. H. (2013). Creativity and technical innovation: Spatial ability's unique role. *Psychological Science, 24,* 1831–1836. https://doi.org/10.1177/0956797613478615.

Keunen, K., Counsell, S. J., & Benders, M. J. (2017). The emergence of functional architecture during early brain development. *Neuroimage, 160,* 2–14. https://doi.org/10.1016/j.neuroimage.2017.01.047.

Kim, D., & Opfer, J. E. (2018). Dynamics and development in number-to-space mapping. *Cognitive Psychology, 107,* 44–66. https://doi.org/10.1016/j .cogpsych.2018.10.001.

Kirschner, P. A., Sweller, J., & Clark, R. E. (2006). Why minimal guidance during instruction does not work: An analysis of the failure of constructivist, discovery, problem-based, experiential, and inquiry-based teaching. *Educational Psychologist, 41*(2), 75–86. https://doi.org/10.1207/ s15326985ep4102_1.

Kline, M. A. (2015). How to learn about teaching: An evolutionary framework for the study of teaching behavior in humans and other animals. *Behavioral and Brain Sciences, 38,* e31. https://doi.org/10.1017/S0140525X14000090.

Konner, M. (2010). *The evolution of childhood: Relationships, emotion, mind.* Harvard University Press.

Konu, D., Turnbull, A., Karapanagiotidis, T., et al. (2020). A role for the ventromedial prefrontal cortex in self-generated episodic social cognition. *Neuroimage, 218,* 116977. https://doi.org/10.1016/j.neuroimage.2020.116977.

Kriegbaum, K., Becker, N., & Spinath, B. (2018). The relative importance of intelligence and motivation as predictors of school achievement: A meta-analysis. *Educational Research Review, 25,* 120–148. https://doi.org/ 10.1016/j.edurev.2018.10.001.

Krubitzer, L. (1995). The organization of neocortex in mammals: Are species differences really so different? *Trends in Neurosciences, 18*(9), 408–417. https://doi.org/10.1016/0166-2236(95)93938-T.

Kuhl, P. K. (2010). Brain mechanisms in early language acquisition. *Neuron, 67* (5), 713–727. https://doi.org/10.1016/j.neuron.2010.08.038.

Kuhl, P. K., Andruski, J. E., Chistovich, I. A. et al. (1997). Cross-language analysis of phonetic units in language addressed to infants. *Science, 277* (5326), 684–686. https://doi.org/10.1126/science.277.5326.684.

Kühn, S., Ritter, S. M., Müller, B. C. et al. (2014). The importance of the default mode network in creativity – A structural MRI study. *The Journal of Creative Behavior, 48*(2), 152–163. https://doi.org/10.1002/jocb.45

Lancy, D. F. (2016). Teaching: Natural or cultural? In D. C. Geary, & D. B. Berch (Eds.), *Evolutionary perspectives on child development and education* (pp. 33–65). Springer.

Leary, M. R., & Buttermore, N. R. (2003). The evolution of the human self: Tracing the natural history of self-awareness. *Journal for the Theory of Social Behaviour, 33*, 365–404. https://doi.org/10.1046/j.1468-5914.2003.00223.x.

LeFevre, J. A., Fast, L., Skwarchuk, S. L. et al. (2010). Pathways to mathematics: Longitudinal predictors of performance. *Child Development, 81*, 1753–1767. https://doi.org/10.1111/j.1467-8624.2010.01508.x.

Legare, C. H. (2017). Cumulative cultural learning: Development and diversity. *Proceedings of the National Academy of Sciences of the United States of America, 114*(30), 7877–7883. https://doi.org/10.1073/pnas.1620743114.

Lehman, H. C. (1946). The exponential increase of man's cultural output. *Social Forces, 25*, 281–290. https://doi.org/10.2307/3005665.

Lenneberg, E. H. (1969). On Explaining Language: The development of language in children can best be understood in the context of developmental biology. *Science, 164*(3880), 635–643. https://doi.org/10.1126/science.164.3880.635.

Leslie, A. M., Friedman, O., & German, T. P. (2004). Core mechanisms in "theory of mind." *Trends in Cognitive Sciences, 8*(12), 528–533. https://doi.org/10.1016/j.tics.2004.10.001.

Lespiau, F., & Tricot, A. (2019). Using primary knowledge: An efficient way to motivate students and promote the learning of formal reasoning. *Educational Psychology Review, 31*, 915–938. https://doi.org/10.1007/s10648-019-09482-4.

Lespiau, F., & Tricot, A. (2022a). Primary vs. secondary knowledge contents in reasoning: Motivated and efficient vs. overburdened. *Acta Psychologica, 227*, 103610. https://doi.org/10.1016/j.actpsy.2022.103610.

Lespiau, F., & Tricot, A. (2022b). Using primary knowledge in unpopular statistics exercises. *Educational Psychology Review, 34*(4), 2297–2322. https://doi.org/10.1007/s10648-022-09699-w.

Levine, S. C., & Pantoja, N. (2021). Development of children's math attitudes: Gender differences, key socializers, and intervention approaches. *Developmental Review, 62*(1), 100997. doi.org/10.1016/j.dr.2021.100997.

Lewis, A. B., & Mayer, R. E. (1987). Students' miscomprehension of relational statements in arithmetic word problems. *Journal of Educational Psychology, 79*, 363–371. https://doi.org/10.1037/0022-0663.79.4.363.

Lewis, A. B. (1989). Training students to represent arithmetic word problems. *Journal of Educational Psychology*, *81*, 521–531. https://doi.org/10.1037/0022-0663.81.4.521

Li, J., Osher, D. E., Hansen, H. A., & Saygin, Z. M. (2020). Innate connectivity patterns drive the development of the visual word form area. *Scientific Reports*, *10*(1), 18039. https://doi.org/10.1038/s41598-020-75015-7.

Libertus, M. E., Halberda, J., & Feigenson, L. (2011). Preschool acuity of the Approximate Number System correlates with math abilities. *Developmental Science*, *14*, 1292–1300. dx.doi.org/10.1111/j.1467-7687.2011.01080.x.

Longo, M. R., & Lourenco, S. F. (2007). Spatial attention and the mental number line: Evidence for characteristic biases and compression. *Neuropsychologia*, *45*, 1400–1407. https://doi.org/10.1016/j.neuropsychologia.2006.11.002.

Lou, H. C., Changeux, J. P., & Rosenstand, A. (2017). Towards a cognitive neuroscience of self- awareness. *Neuroscience & Biobehavioral Reviews*, *83* (1), 765–773. https://doi.org/10.1016/j.neubiorev.2016.04.004.

Lubinski, D. (2000). Scientific and social significance of assessing individual differences: "Sinking shafts at a few critical points." *Annual Review of Psychology*, *51*, 405–444. https://doi.org/10.1146/annurev.psych.51.1.405.

Lukas, D., & Clutton-Brock, T. H. (2018). Social complexity and kinship in animal societies. *Ecology Letters*, *21*(8), 1129–1134. https://doi.org/10.1111/ele.13079.

Lyons, I. M., & Beilock, S. L. (2012). When math hurts: Math anxiety predicts pain network activation in anticipation of doing math. *PLoS ONE*, *7*(10), e48076. https://doi.org/10.1371/journal.pone.0048076.

Ma, X. (1999). A meta-analysis of the relationship between anxiety toward mathematics and achievement in mathematics. *Journal for Research in Mathematics Education*, *30*(5), 520–540. https://doi.org/10.2307/749772.

Ma, X., & Xu, J. (2004). The causal ordering of mathematics anxiety and mathematics achievement: A longitudinal panel analysis. *Journal of Adolescence*, *27*(2), 165–179. https://doi.org/10.1016/j.adolescence.2003.11.003.

Mac Arthur, R. H., & Wilson, E. O. (1967). *The theory of island biogeography.* Princeton University Press.

Mackintosh, N. J., & Bennett, E. S. (2003). The fractionation of working memory maps onto different components of intelligence. *Intelligence*, *31* (6), 519–531. https://doi.org/10.1016/S0160-2896(03)00052-7.

Malt, B. C. (1995). Category coherence in cross-cultural perspective. *Cognitive Psychology*, *29*(2), 85–148. doi.org/10.1006/cogp.1995.1013.

Malthus, T. R. (1798). *An essay on the principle of population as it affects the future improvement of society with remarks on the speculations of*

*Mr. Godwin, M. Condorcet, and other writers*. Printed for J. Johnson, in St. Paul's church-yard.

Mancuso, L., Cavuoti-Cabanillas, S., Liloia, D. et al. (2022). Tasks activating the default mode network map multiple functional systems. *Brain Structure and Function*, *227*(5), 1711–1734. https://doi.org/10.1007/s00429-022-02467-0.

Mann, V. A. (1984). Reading skill and language skill. *Developmental Review, 4* (1), 1–15. https://doi.org/10.1016/0273-2297(84)90014-5.

Margett-Jordan, T., Falcon, R. G., & Witherington, D. C. (2017). The development of preschoolers' living kinds concept: A longitudinal study. *Child Development*, *88*(4), 1350–1367. https://doi.org/10.1111/cdev.12709.

Marron, T. R., Lerner, Y., Berant, E. et al. (2018). Chain free association, creativity, and the default mode network. *Neuropsychologia*, *118*, 40–58. https://doi.org/10.1016/j.neuropsychologia.2018.03.018.

Marsh, H. W., Hau, K.-T., Artelt, C., Baumert, J., & Peschar, J. L. (2006). OECD's brief self- report measure of educational psychology's most useful affective constructs: Cross-cultural, psychometric comparisons across 25 countries. *International Journal of Testing*, *6*, 311–360. https://doi.org/10.1207/s15327574ijt0604_1.

Marsh, H. W., & Martin, A. J. (2011). Academic self-concept and academic achievement: Relations and causal ordering. *British Journal of Educational Psychology*, *81*, 59–77. https://doi.org/10.1348/000709910X503501.

Marsh, H. W., & Shavelson, R. (1985). Self-concept: Its multifaceted, hierarchical structure. *Educational Psychologist*, *20*, 107–123. https://doi.org/10.1207/s15326985ep2003_1.

Martin, P. S. (1973). The discovery of America: The first Americans may have swept the Western Hemisphere and decimated its fauna in 1000 years. *Science*, *179*(4077), 969–974. https://doi.org/10.1126/science.179.4077.969.

Martin, A. E., & Slepian, M. L. (2021). The primacy of gender: Gendered cognition underlies the big two dimensions of social cognition. *Perspectives on Psychological Science*, *16*(6), 1143–1158. https://doi.org/10.1177/1745691620904961.

Martin-Ordas, G. (2020). It is about time: Conceptual and experimental evaluation of the temporal cognitive mechanisms in mental time travel. *Wiley Interdisciplinary Reviews: Cognitive Science*, *11*(6), e1530. https://doi.org/10.1002/wcs.1530.

Matchin, W. G. (2018). A neuronal retuning hypothesis of sentence-specificity in Broca's area. *Psychonomic Bulletin & Review*, *25*, 1682–1694. https://doi.org/10.3758/s13423-017-1377-6.

Mayer, R. E. (2004). Should there be a three-strikes rule against pure discovery learning? *American Psychologist, 59*(1), 14–19. https://doi.org/10.1037/0003-066X.59.1.14.

McCandliss, B. D., Cohen, L., & Dehaene, S. (2003). The visual word form area: Expertise for reading in the fusiform gyrus. *Trends in Cognitive Sciences, 7*(7), 293–299. https://doi.org/10.1016/S1364-6613(03)00134-7.

McGrew, K. S. (2009). CHC theory and the human cognitive abilities project: Standing on the shoulders of the giants of psychometric intelligence research. *Intelligence, 37*(1), 1–10. https://doi.org/10.1016/j.intell.2008.08.004.

McNally, R. J. (1987). Preparedness and phobias: A review. *Psychological Bulletin, 101*(2), 283–303. https://doi.org/10.1037/0033-2909.101.2.283.

Medin, D. L., & Atran, S. (2004). The native mind: Biological categorization and reasoning in development and across cultures. *Psychological Review, 111*(4), 960–983. https://doi.org/10.1037/0033-295X.111.4.960.

Medin, D. L., Ross, N. O., Atran, S. et al. (2006). Folkbiology of freshwater fish. *Cognition, 99*(3), 237–273. https://doi.org/10.1016/j.cognition.2003.12.005.

Menon, V., & Chang, H. (2021). Emerging neurodevelopmental perspectives on mathematical learning. *Developmental Review, 60*, 100964. https://doi.org/10.1016/j.dr.2021.100964.

Menon, V., & D'Esposito, M. (2022). The role of PFC networks in cognitive control and executive function. *Neuropsychopharmacology, 47*(1), 90–103. https://doi.org/10.1038/s41386-021-01152-w.

Menon, V., & Uddin, L. Q. (2010). Saliency, switching, attention and control: A network model of insula function. *Brain Structure and Function, 214*, 655–667. https://doi.org/10.1007/s00429-010-0262-0.

Mesoudi, A., & Thornton, A. (2018). What is cumulative cultural evolution?. *Proceedings of the Royal Society B, 285*(1880), 20180712. https://doi.org/10.1098/rspb.2018.0712.

Meyer, L. A. (1984). Long-term academic effects of the direct instruction project follow through. *The Elementary School Journal, 84*, 380–394. https://doi.org/10.1086/461371.

Meyer, L. A., Gersten, R. M., & Gutkin, J. (1983). Direct instruction: A project follow through success story in an inner-city school. *The Elementary School Journal, 84*, 241–252. https://doi.org/10.1086/461360.

Middleton, W. K. (1963). The place of Torricelli in the history of the barometer. *Isis, 54*(1), 11–28. www.jstor.org/stable/228726.

Milner, A. D., & Goodale, M. A. (2006). *The visual brain in action* (2nd ed). Oxford University Press. https://doi.org/10.1093/acprof:oso/9780198524724.001.0001.

Mithen, S. (1996). *The prehistory of the mind: The cognitive origins of art and science*. Thames and Hudson.

Mix, K. S. (2019). Why are spatial skill and mathematics related? *Child Development Perspectives*, *13*, 121–126. https://doi.org/10.1111/cdep12323.

Miyake, A., & Friedman, N. P. (2012). The nature and organization of individual differences in executive functions: Four general conclusions. *Current Directions in Psychological Science*, *21*(1), 8–14. https://doi.org/10.1177/0963721411429458.

Molnar-Szakacs, I., & Uddin, L. Q. (2022). Anterior insula as a gatekeeper of executive control. *Neuroscience & Biobehavioral Reviews*, *139*, 104736. https://doi.org/10.1016/j.neubiorev.2022.104736.

Monosov, I. E., Haber, S. N., Leuthardt, E. C., & Jezzini, A. (2020). Anterior cingulate cortex and the control of dynamic behavior in primates. *Current Biology*, *30*(23), R1442–R1454. https://doi.org/10.1016/j.cub.2020.10.009.

Mou, Y., & vanMarle, K. (2014). Two core systems of numerical representation in infants. *Developmental Review*, *34*(1), 1–25. https://doi.org/10.1016/j.dr.2013.11.001.

Moulton, E., Bouhali, F., Monzalvo, K. et al. (2019). Connectivity between the visual word form area and the parietal lobe improves after the first year of reading instruction: A longitudinal MRI study in children. *Brain Structure and Function*, *224*, 1519–1536. https://doi.org/10.1007/s00429-019-01855-3.

Murray, C. (2003). *Human accomplishment: The pursuit of excellence in the arts and sciences, 800 B.C. to 1950*. HarperCollins.

Murray, E. A., Wise, S. P., & Graham, K. S. (2018). Representational specializations of the hippocampus in phylogenetic perspective. *Neuroscience Letters*, *680*(1), 4–12. https://doi.org/10.1016/j.neulet.2017.04.065.

Mussolin, C., Nys, J., Leybaert, J., & Content, A. (2016). How approximate and exact number skills are related to each other across development: A review. *Developmental Review*, *39*, 1–15. https://doi.org/10.1016/j.dr.2014.11.001.

Neisser, U. (1988). Five kinds of self-knowledge. *Philosophical Psychology*, *1*, 35–59. https://doi.org/10.1080/09515088808572924.

Newcombe, N. S., Uttal, D. H., & Sauter, M. (2013). Spatial development. In P. Zelazo (Ed.), *Oxford handbook of developmental psychology* (pp. 564–590). Oxford University Press.

Newton, I. (1995). *The principia* (A. Motte, Trans.). Prometheus Books. (Original work published in 1687).

Nguyen, V., Versyp, O., Cox, C., & Fusaroli, R. (2022). A systematic review and Bayesian meta-analysis of the development of turn taking in adult–child vocal interactions. *Child Development*, *93*(4), 1181–1200. https://doi.org/10.1111/cdev.13754.

Nicolson, R. I., & Fawcett, A. J. (2019). Development of dyslexia: The delayed neural commitment framework. *Frontiers in Behavioral Neuroscience, 13*, 112. https://doi.org/10.3389/fnbeh.2019.00112.

Northcutt, R. G., & Kaas, J. H. (1995). The emergence and evolution of mammalian neocortex. *Trends in Neurosciences, 18*(9), 373–379. https://doi.org/10.1016/0166-2236(95)93932-N.

Núñez, R. E. (2008). Reading between the number lines. *Science, 321*(5894), 1293–1294. https://doi.org/10.1126/science.321.5894.1293.

Öhman, A., & Mineka, S. (2001). Fears, phobias, and preparedness: Toward an evolved module of fear and fear learning. *Psychological Review, 108*(3), 483–522. https://doi.org/10.1037/0033-295X.108.3.483.

O'Keefe, J., & Nadel, L. (1978). *The hippocampus as a cognitive map*. Oxford University Press.

O'Leary, D. D. M., Schlaggar, B. L., & Tuttle, R. (1994). Specification of neocortical areas and thalamocortical connections. *Annual Review of Neuroscience, 17*, 419–439. https://doi.org/10.1146/annurev.ne.17.030194.002223.

Park, G., Lubinski, D., & Benbow, C. P. (2007). Contrasting intellectual patterns predict creativity in the arts and sciences: Tracking intellectually precocious youth over 25 years. *Psychological Science, 18*(11), 948–952. https://doi.org/10.1111/j.1467-9280.2007.02007.

Pascalis, O., de Haan, M., & Nelson, C. A. (2002). In face processing species-specific during the first year of life? *Science, 296*(5571), 1321–1323. https://doi.org/10.1126/science.1070223.

Paulesu, E., Démonet, J. F., Fazio, F. et al. (2001). Dyslexia: Cultural diversity and biological unity. *Science, 291*(5511), 2165–2167. https://doi.org/10.1126/science.1057179.

Penn, D. C., Holyoak, K. J., & Povinelli, D. J. (2008). Darwin's mistake: Explaining the discontinuity between human and nonhuman minds. *Behavioral and Brain Sciences, 31*(2), 109–130. https://doi.org/10.1017/S0140525X08003543.

Peter, V., Kalashnikova, M., Santos, A., & Burnham, D. (2016). Mature neural responses to infant-directed speech but not adult-directed speech in pre-verbal infants. *Scientific Reports, 6*(1), 34273. https://doi.org/10.1038/srep34273.

Piazza, M., Pinel, P., Le Bihan, D., & Dehaene, S. (2007). A magnitude code common to numerosities and number symbols in human intraparietal cortex. *Neuron, 53*, 293–305. https://doi.org/10.1016/j.neuron.2006.11.022.

Pinker, S. (1994). *The language instinct*. William Morrow.

Pinker, S. (2004). *The blank slate: The modern denial of human nature.* Viking.

Pinker, S., & Bloom, P. (1990). Natural language and natural selection. *Behavioral and Brain Sciences*, *13*(4), 707–784. https://doi.org/10.1017/S0140525X00081061.

Pinsof, D., Sears, D. O., & Haselton, M. G. (2023). Strange bedfellows: The Alliance Theory of political belief systems. *Psychological Inquiry*, *34*(3), 139–160. https://doi.org/10.1080/1047840X.2023.2274433.

Pletzer, B., Kronbichler, M., Nuerk, H. C., & Kerschbaum, H. H. (2015). Mathematics anxiety reduces default mode network deactivation in response to numerical tasks. *Frontiers in Human Neuroscience*, *9*, 202. https://doi.org/10.3389/fnhum.2015.00202.

Poropat, A. E. (2009). A meta-analysis of the five-factor model of personality and academic performance. *Psychological Bulletin*, *135*(2), 322–338. https://doi.org/10.1037/a0014996.

Posner, M. I. (2023). The evolution and future development of attention networks. *Journal of Intelligence*, *11*(6), 98. https://doi.org/10.3390/jintelligence11060098.

Posner, M. I., & Rothbart, M. K. (2009). Toward a physical basis of attention and self-regulation. *Physics of Life Reviews*, *6*(2), 103–120. https://doi.org/10.1016/j.plrev.2009.02.001.

Potts, R. (1998). Variability selection in hominid evolution. *Evolutionary Anthropology*, *7*(3), 81–96. https://doi.org/10.1002/(SICI)1520-6505(1998)7:3<81::AID-EVAN3>3.0.CO;2-A.

Povinelli, D. J. (2000). *Folk physics for apes: The chimpanzee's theory of how the world works.* Oxford University Press. https://doi.org/10.1093/acprof:oso/9780198572190.001.0001.

Power, J. D., Schlaggar, B. L., Lessov-Schlaggar, C. N., & Petersen, S. E. (2013). Evidence for hubs in human functional brain networks. *Neuron*, *79*, 798–813. https://doi.org/10.1016/j.neuron.2013.07.035.

Preuss, T. M., & Wise, S. P. (2022). Evolution of prefrontal cortex. *Neuropsychopharmacology*, *47*(1), 3–19. https://doi.org/10.1038/s41386-021-01076-5.

Price, C. J., & Mechelli, A. (2005). Reading and reading disturbance. *Current Opinion in Neurobiology*, *15*(2), 231–238. https://doi.org/10.1016/j.conb.2005.03.003.

Pugh, K. R., Shaywitz, B. A., Shaywitz, S. E. et al. (1997). Predicting reading performance from neuroimaging profiles: The cerebral basis of phonological effects in printed word identification. *Journal of Experimental Psychology: Human Perception and Performance*, *23*(2), 299–318. https://doi.org/10.1037/0096-1523.23.2.299.

Qin, S., Cho, S., Chen, T. et al. (2014). Hippocampal-neocortical functional reorganization underlies children's cognitive development. *Nature Neuroscience, 17*, 1263–1269. https://doi.org/10.1038/nn.3788.

Raichle, M. E. (2015). The brain's default mode network. *Annual Review of Neuroscience, 38*, 433–447. https://doi.org/abs/10.1146/annurev-neuro-071013-014030.

Rakic, P. (1988). Specification of cerebral cortical areas. *Science, 241*(4862), 170–176. www.jstor.org/stable/1701135.

Ramani, G. B., Rowe, M. L., Eason, S. H., & Leech, K. A. (2015). Math talk during informal learning activities in Head Start families. *Cognitive Development, 35*, 15–33. https://doi.org/10.1016/j.cogdev.2014.11.002.

Ramirez, F. O., & Boli, J. (1987). The political construction of mass schooling: European origins and worldwide institutionalization. *Sociology of Education, 60*(1), 2–17. https://doi.org/10.2307/2112615.

Ramirez, G., Shaw, S. T., & Maloney, E. A. (2018). Math anxiety: Past research, promising interventions, and a new interpretation framework. *Educational Psychologist, 53*(3), 145–164. https://doi.org/10.1080/00461520.2018.1447384.

Redick, T. S., Shipstead, Z., Meier, M. E. et al. (2016). Cognitive predictors of a common multitasking ability: Contributions from working memory, attention control, and fluid intelligence. *Journal of Experimental Psychology: General, 145*(11), 1473–1492. https://doi.org/10.1037/xge0000219.

Reynaud, E., Lesourd, M., Navarro, J., & Osiurak, F. (2016). On the neurocognitive origins of human tool use: A critical review of neuroimaging data. *Neuroscience & Biobehavioral Reviews, 64*(1), 421–437. https://doi.org/10.1016/j.neubiorev.2016.03.009.

Richerson, P., & Boyd, R. (2005). *Not by genes alone: How culture transformed human evolution*. University of Chicago Press.

Richlan, F., Kronbichler, M., & Wimmer, H. (2011). Meta-analyzing brain dysfunctions in dyslexic children and adults. *Neuroimage, 56*(3), 1735–1742. https://doi.org/10.1016/j.neuroimage.2011.02.040.

Richmond-Rakerd, L. S., D'Souza, S., Andersen, S. H. et al. (2020). Clustering of health, crime and social-welfare inequality in 4 million citizens from two nations. *Nature Human Behaviour, 4*, 255–264. https://doi.org/10.1038/s41562-019-0810-4.

Riek, B. M., Mania, E. W., & Gaertner, S. L. (2006). Intergroup threat and outgroup attitudes: A meta-analytic review. *Personality and Social Psychology Review, 10*(4), 336–353. https://doi.org/10.1207/s15327957pspr1004_4.

Ritchie, S. J., & Bates, T. C. (2013). Enduring links from childhood mathematics and reading achievement to adult socioeconomic status. *Psychological Science, 24*(7), 1301–1308. https://doi.org/10.1177/0956797612466268.

Rivera, S. M., Reiss, A. L., Eckert, M. A., & Menon, V. (2005). Developmental changes in mental arithmetic: Evidence for increased functional specialization in the left inferior parietal cortex. *Cerebral Cortex, 15*, 1779–1790. https://doi.org/10.1093/cercor/bhi05.

Rivera-Batiz, F. L. (1992). Quantitative literacy and the likelihood of employment among young adults in the United States. *Journal of Human Resources, 27*(2), 313–328. www.jstor.org/stable/145737.

Rouder, J. N., & Geary, D. C. (2014). Children's cognitive representation of the mathematical number line. *Developmental Science, 17*, 525–536. https://doi.org/10.1111/desc.12166.

Rousseau, J.-J. (1979). *Emile: Or, on education* (A. Bloom, Trans.). Basic Books. (Original work published 1762).

Roy, D. S., Zhang, Y., Halassa, M. M., & Feng, G. (2022). Thalamic subnetworks as units of function. *Nature Neuroscience, 25*(2), 140–153. https://doi.org/10.1038/s41593-021-00996-1.

Rozin, P. (1976). The evolution of intelligence and access to the cognitive unconscious. In J. M. Sprague, & A. N. Epstein (Eds.), *Progress in psychobiology and physiological psychology* (Vol. 6, pp. 245–280). Academic Press.

Rueter, A. R., Abram, S. V., MacDonald III, A. W., Rustichini, A., & DeYoung, C. G. (2018). The goal priority network as a neural substrate of conscientiousness. *Human Brain Mapping, 39*(9), 3574–3585. https://doi.org/10.1002/hbm.24195.

Rugg, M. D., & Vilberg, K. L. (2013). Brain networks underlying episodic memory retrieval. *Current Opinion in Neurobiology, 23*(2), 255–260. https://doi.org/10.1016/j.conb.2012.11.005.

Ryan, R. M., & Deci, E. L. (2017). *Self-determination theory: Basic psychological needs in motivation, development, and wellness.* Guilford Press.

Sakamoto, A., Goyette, K. A., & Kim, C. (2009). Socioeconomic attainments of Asian Americans. *Annual Review of Sociology, 35*, 255–276. http://doi.org/10.1146/annurev-soc-070308-115958.

Sampaio-Baptista, C., & Johansen-Berg, H. (2017). White matter plasticity in the adult brain. *Neuron, 96*(6), 1239–1251. https://doi.org/10.1016/j.neuron.2017.11.026.

Santarnecchi, E., Emmendorfer, A., & Pascual-Leone, A. (2017). Dissecting the parieto-frontal correlates of fluid intelligence: A comprehensive ALE meta-analysis study. *Intelligence, 63*, 9–28. https://doi.org/10.1016/j.intell.2017.04.008.

Sassenberg, T. A., Burton, P. C., Mwilambwe-Tshilobo, L. et al. (2023). Conscientiousness associated with efficiency of the salience/ventral attention network: Replication in three samples using individualized parcellation. *NeuroImage, 272*, 120081. https://doi.org/10.1016/j.neuroimage.2023.120081.

Saygin, Z. M., Osher, D. E., Norton, E. S. et al. (2016). Connectivity precedes function in the development of the visual word form area. *Nature Neuroscience, 19*(9), 1250–1255. https://doi.org/10.1038/nn.4354.

Scarr, S. (1992). Developmental theories of the 1990s: Developmental and individual differences. *Child Development, 63*(1), 1–19. https://doi.org/10.1111/j.1467-8624.1992.tb03591.x.

Schimmelpfennig, J., Topczewski, J., Zajkowski, W., & Jankowiak-Siuda, K. (2023). The role of the salience network in cognitive and affective deficits. *Frontiers in Human Neuroscience, 17*, 1133367. https://doi.org/10.3389/fnhum.2023.1133367.

Schlaggar, B. L., & McCandliss, B. D. (2007). Development of neural systems for reading. *Annual Review of Neuroscience, 30*, 475–503. https://doi.org/10.1146/annurev.neuro.28.061604.135645.

Schlegel, A. A., Rudelson, J. J., & Tse, P. U. (2012). White matter structure changes as adults learn a second language. *Journal of Cognitive Neuroscience, 24*(8), 1664–1670. https://doi.org/10.1162/jocn_a_00240.

Schmidt, F. L., & Hunter, J. (2004). General mental ability in the world of work: Occupational attainment and job performance. *Journal of Personality and Social Psychology, 86*(1), 162–173. https://doi.org/10.1037/0022-3514.86.1.162.

Schneider, M., & Preckel, F. (2017). Variables associated with achievement in higher education: A systematic review of meta-analyses. *Psychological Bulletin, 143*(6), 565–600. https://doi.org/10.1037/bul0000098.

Schöpf, V., Kasprian, G., Brugger, P. C., & Prayer, D. (2012). Watching the fetal brain at "rest." *International Journal of Developmental Neuroscience, 30*(1), 11–17. https://doi.org/10.1016/j.ijdevneu.2011.10.006.

Schurz, M., Radua, J., Aichhorn, M., Richlan, F., & Perner, J. (2014). Fractionating theory of mind: A meta-analysis of functional brain imaging studies. *Neuroscience & Biobehavioral Reviews, 42*, 9–34. https://doi.org/10.1016/j.neubiorev.2014.01.009.

Seligman, M. E. (1971). Phobias and preparedness. *Behavior Therapy, 2*(3), 307–320. https://doi.org/10.1016/S0005-7894(71)80064-3.

Setoh, P., Wu, D., Baillargeon, R., & Gelman, R. (2013). Young infants have biological expectations about animals. *Proceedings of the National Academy of Sciences of the United States of America, 110*(40), 15937–15942. https://doi.org/10.1073/pnas.1314075110.

Shavelson, R. J., Hubner, J. J., & Stanton, G. C. (1976). Self-concept: Validation of construct interpretations. *Review of Educational Research, 46*, 407–441. https://doi.org/10.3102/00346543046003407.

Siegler, R. S., & Braithwaite, D. W. (2017). Numerical development. *Annual Review of Psychology*, *68*, 187–213. https://doi.org/100.1146/annurev-psych-010416-044101.

Siegler, R. S., & Opfer, J. E. (2003). The development of numerical estimation: Evidence for multiple representations of numerical quantity. *Psychological Science*, *14*, 237–250. https://doi.org/10.1111/1467-9280.02438.

Siegler, R. S., Thompson, C. A., & Schneider, M. (2011). An integrated theory of whole number and fractions development. *Cognitive Psychology*, *62*, 273–296. https://doi.org/10.1016/j.cogpsych.2011.03.001.

Simonton, D. K. (2003). Scientific creativity as constrained stochastic behavior: The integration of product, person, and process perspectives. *Psychological Bulletin*, *129*(4), 475–494. https://doi.org/10.1037/0033-2909.129.4.475.

Skipper, J. I., Goldin-Meadow, S., Nusbaum, H. C., & Small, S. L. (2007). Speech-associated gestures, Broca's area, and the human mirror system. *Brain and Language*, *101*(3), 260–277. https://doi.org/10.1016/j.bandl.2007.02.008.

Slater, A., Mattock, A., & Brown, E. (1990). Size constancy at birth: Newborn infants' responses to retinal and real size. *Journal of Experimental Child Psychology*, *49*, 314–322. https://doi.org/10.1016/0022-0965(90)90061-C.

Sliwa, J., & Freiwald, W. A. (2017). A dedicated network for social interaction processing in the primate brain. *Science*, *356*(6339), 745–749. https://doi.org/10.1126/science.aam6383.

Slusser, E. B., Santiago, R. T., & Barth, H. C. (2013). Developmental change in numerical estimation. *Journal of Experimental Psychology: General*, *142*, 193–208. https://doi.org/10.1037/a0028560.

Smaers, J. B., & Vanier, D. R. (2019). Brain size expansion in primates and humans is explained by a selective modular expansion of the cortico-cerebellar system. *Cortex*, *118*, 292–305. https://doi.org/10.1016/j.cortex.2019.04.023.

Smallwood, J., Bernhardt, B. C., Leech, R. et al. (2021). The default mode network in cognition: A topographical perspective. *Nature Reviews Neuroscience*, *22*(8), 503–513. https://doi.org/10.1038/s41583-021-00474-4.

Sniekers, S., Stringer, S., Watanabe, K. et al. (2017). Genome-wide association meta-analysis of 78,308 individuals identifies new loci and genes influencing human intelligence. *Nature Genetics*, *49*(7), 1107–1112. https://doi.org/10.1038/ng.3869.

Spearman, C. (1904). "General intelligence," objectively determined and measured. *The American Journal of Psychology*, *15*(2), 201–292. https://doi.org/10.2307/1412107.

Spelke, E. S. (2017). Core knowledge, language, and number. *Language Learning and Development*, *13*(2), 147–170. https://doi.org/10.1080/15475441.2016.1263572.

Spelke, E. S., Breinlinger, K., Macomber, J., & Jacobson, K. (1992). Origins of knowledge. *Psychological Review*, *99*(4), 605–632. https://doi.org/10.1037/0033-295X.99.4.605.

Spelke, E., Lee, S. A., & Izard, V. (2010). Beyond core knowledge: Natural geometry. *Cognitive Science*, *34*, 863–884. https://doi.org/10.1111/j.1551-6709.2010.01110.x.

Spielmann, J., Yoon, H. J. R., Ayoub, M. et al. (2022). An in-depth review of conscientiousness and educational issues. *Educational Psychology Review*, *34*(4), 2745–2781. https://doi.org/10.1007/s10648-022-09693-2.

Srinivasan, S., Bettella, F., Frei, O. et al. (2018). Enrichment of genetic markers of recent human evolution in educational and cognitive traits. *Scientific Reports*, *8*(1), 12585. https://doi.org/10.1038/s41598-018-30387-9.

Stanek, K. C., & Ones, D. S. (2023). Meta-analytic relations between personality and cognitive ability. *Proceedings of the National Academy of Sciences of the United States of America*, *120*(23), e2212794120. https://doi.org/10.1073/pnas.2212794120.

Stanovich, K. E. (1988). Explaining the differences between the dyslexic and the garden-variety poor reader: The phonological-core variable-difference model. *Journal of Learning Disabilities*, *21*(10), 590–604. https://doi.org/10.1177/002221948802101003.

Stanovich, K. E., West, R. F., & Toplak, M. E. (2016). *The rationality quotient: Toward a test of rational thinking*. The MIT Press.

Stebbins, L. B. (1977). *Education as experimentation: A planned variation model* (Vol. 4). University Press of America.

Sternberg, R. J. (2021). Transformational creativity: The link between creativity, wisdom, and the solution of global problems. *Philosophies*, *6*(3), 75. https://doi.org/10.3390/philosophies6030075.

Stevens, W. D., Kravitz, D. J., Peng, C. S., Tessler, M. H., & Martin, A. (2017). Privileged functional connectivity between the visual word form area and the language system. *Journal of Neuroscience*, *37*(21), 5288–5297. https://doi.org/10.1523/JNEUROSCI.0138-17.2017.

Stevenson, H., & Stigler, J. W. (1992). *Learning gap: Why our schools are failing and what we can learn from Japanese and Chinese education*. Summit Books.

Suddendorf, T., & Corballis, M. C. (2007). The evolution of foresight: What is mental time travel, and is it unique to humans? *Behavioral and Brain Sciences*, *30*(3), 299–313. https://doi.org/10.1017/S0140525X07001975.

Sullivan, J., & Barner, D. (2014). Inference and association in children's early numerical estimation. *Child Development*, *85*(4), 1740–1755. https://doi.org/10.1111/cdev.12211.

Summerfield, C., Luyckx, F., & Sheahan, H. (2020). Structure learning and the posterior parietal cortex. *Progress in Neurobiology, 184,* 101717. https://doi .org/10.1016/j.pneurobio.2019.101717.

Supekar, K., Iuculano, T., Chen, L., & Menon, V. (2015). Remediation of childhood math anxiety and associated neural circuits through cognitive tutoring. *Journal of Neuroscience, 35*(36), 12574–12583. https://doi.org/ 10.1523/JNEUROSCI.0786-15.2015.

Sweller, J., & Cooper, G. A. (1985). The use of worked examples as a substitute for problem solving in learning algebra. *Cognition and Instruction, 2*(1), 59–89. https://doi.org/10.1207/s1532690xci0201_3.

Sweller, J., van Merriënboer, J. J., & Paas, F. (2019). Cognitive architecture and instructional design: 20 years later. *Educational Psychology Review, 31,* 261–292. https://doi.org/10.1007/s10648-019-09465-5.

Szkudlarek, E., & Brannon, E. M. (2017). Does the approximate number system serve as a foundation for symbolic mathematics? *Language Learning and Development, 13,* 171–190. https://doi.org/10.1080/15475441.2016.1263573.

Szűcs, D., & Myers, T. (2017). A critical analysis of design, facts, bias and inference in the approximate number system training literature: A systematic review. *Trends in Neuroscience and Education, 6,* 187–203. https://doi.org/ 10.1016/j.tine.2016.11.002.

Thompson, P. M., Cannon, T. D., Narr, K. L. et al. (2001). Genetic influences on brain structure. *Nature Neuroscience, 4*(12), 1253–1258. https://doi.org/ 10.1038/nn758.

Thurstone, L. L., & Thurstone, T. G. (1941). Factorial studies of intelligence. *Psychometric Monographs* (No. 2). University of Chicago Press.

Tomasello, M. (1999). *The cultural origins of human cognition.* Harvard University Press. https://doi.org/10.2307/j.ctvjsf4jc.

Toub, T. S., Rajan, V., Golinkoff, R. M., & Hirsh-Pasek, K. (2016). Guided play: A solution to the play versus learning dichotomy. In D. C. Geary, & D. B. Berch (Eds.), *Evolutionary perspectives on child development and education* (pp. 117–141). Springer.

Tulving, E. (2002). Episodic memory: From mind to brain. *Annual Review of Psychology, 53,* 1–25. https://doi.org/10.1146/annurev.psych.53.100901 .135114.

Turchin, P. (2009). A theory for formation of large empires. *Journal of Global History, 4*(2), 191–217. https://doi.org/10.1017/S174002280900312X.

Turchin, P., Currie, T. E., Turner, E. A., & Gavrilets, S. (2013). War, space, and the evolution of Old World complex societies. *Proceedings of the National Academy of Sciences of the United States of America, 110*(41), 16384–16389. https://doi.org/10.1073/pnas.1308825110.

Turk, E., Van Den Heuvel, M. I., Benders, M. J. et al. (2019). Functional connectome of the fetal brain. *Journal of Neuroscience, 39*(49), 9716–9724. https://doi.org/10.1523/JNEUROSCI.2891-18.2019.

Turkeltaub, P. E., Gareau, L., Flowers, D. L., Zeffiro, T. A., & Eden, G. F. (2003). Development of neural mechanisms for reading. *Nature Neuroscience, 6*(7), 767–773. https://doi.org/10.1038/nn1065.

Uddin, L. Q. (2015). Salience processing and insular cortical function and dysfunction. *Nature Reviews Neuroscience, 16*(1), 55–61. https://doi.org/10.1038/nrn3857.

Udochi, A. L., Blain, S. D., Sassenberg, T. A. et al. (2022). Activation of the default network during a theory of mind task predicts individual differences in agreeableness and social cognitive ability. *Cognitive, Affective, & Behavioral Neuroscience, 22*, 383–402. https://doi.org/10.3758/s13415-021-00955-0.

Ünal, Z. E., Ala, A. M., Kartal, G., Özel, S., & Geary, D. C. (2023). Visual and symbolic representations as a component of algebraic reasoning. *Journal of Numerical Cognition, 9*(2), 327–345. https://doi.org/10.5964/jnc.11151.

Unsworth, N., Fukuda, K., Awh, E., & Vogel, E. K. (2014). Working memory and fluid intelligence: Capacity, attention control, and secondary memory retrieval. *Cognitive Psychology, 71*, 1–26. https://doi.org/10.1016/j.cogpsych.2014.01.003.

Valentine, J. C., DuBois, D. L., & Cooper, H. (2004). The relation between self-beliefs and academic achievement: A meta-analytic review. *Educational Psychologist, 39*, 111–133. https://doi.org/10.1207/s15326985ep3902_3.

van Garderen, D., Scheuermann, A., & Jackson, C. (2013). Examining how students with diverse abilities use diagrams to solve mathematics word problems. *Learning Disability Quarterly, 36*(3), 145–160. https://doi.org/10.1177/0731948712438558.

Vrba, E. (1996). The fossil record of African antelopes (Mammalia, Bovidae) in relation to human evolution and paleoclimate. In E. S. Vrba, G. H. Denton, T. C. Partridge, & L. H. Burckle (Eds.), *Paleoclimate and evolution, with emphasis on human origins* (pp. 385–424). Yale University Press.

Wagner, J., & Rusconi, E. (2023). Causal involvement of the left angular gyrus in higher functions as revealed by transcranial magnetic stimulation: A systematic review. *Brain Structure and Function, 228*(1), 169–196. https://doi.org/10.1007/s00429-022-02576-w.

Walberg, H. J. (1984). Improving the productivity of America's schools. *Educational Leadership, 41*(8), 19–27.

Wallace, A. R. (1869). Geological climate and origin of species. *London Quarterly Review, 126*(252), 187–205.

Wang, Z., Hart, S. A., Kovas, Y. et al. (2014). Who is afraid of math? Two sources of genetic variance for mathematical anxiety. *Journal of Child Psychology and Psychiatry*, *55*(9), 1056–1064. https://doi.org/10.1111/jcpp.12224

Wang, S., Zhao, Y., Li, J. et al. (2019). Brain structure links trait conscientiousness to academic performance. *Scientific Reports*, *9*(1), 12168. https://doi.org/10.1038/s41598-019-48704-1.

Wang, Z., Rimfeld, K., Shakeshaft, N., Schofield, K., & Malanchini, M. (2020). The longitudinal role of mathematics anxiety in mathematics development: Issues of gender differences and domain-specificity. *Journal of Adolescence*, *80*, 220–232. https://doi.org/10.1016/j.adolescence.2020.03.003.

Wei, Y., de Lange, S. C., Scholtens, L. H. et al. (2019). Genetic mapping and evolutionary analysis of human-expanded cognitive networks. *Nature Communications*, *10*(1), 4839. https://doi.org/10.1038/s41467-019-12764-8.

Wellman, H. M., & Gelman, S. A. (1992). Cognitive development: Foundational theories of core domains. *Annual Review of Psychology*, *43*, 337–375. https://doi.org/10.1146/annurev.ps.43.020192.002005.

West, B. H., Griesbach, E. N., Taylor, J. D., & Taylor, L. T. (1982). *The Prentice-Hall encyclopedia of mathematics*. Prentice-Hall.

Whiten, A., & Van Schaik, C. P. (2007). The evolution of animal "cultures" and social intelligence. *Philosophical Transactions of the Royal Society B: Biological Sciences*, *362*(1480), 603–620. https://doi.org/10.1098/rstb.2006.1998.

Williams, G. C. (1957). Pleiotropy, natural selection and the evolution of senescence. *Evolution*, *11*(4), 398–411. https://doi.org/10.1111/j.1558-5646.1957.tb02911.x.

Winegard, B., Winegard, B., & Geary, D. C. (2018a). The status competition model of cultural production. *Evolutionary Behavioral Science*, *4*(4), 351–371. https://doi.org/10.1007/s40806-018-0147-7.

Winegard, B., Winegard, B., & Geary, D. C. (2018b). The evolution of expertise. In K. A. Ericsson (Ed.), *Cambridge handbook of expertise and expert performance* (2nd ed., pp. 40–48). Cambridge University Press.

Witt, S. T., van Ettinger-Veenstra, H., Salo, T., Riedel, M. C., & Laird, A. R. (2021). What executive function network is that? An image-based meta-analysis of network labels. *Brain Topography*, *34*(5), 598–607. https://doi.org/10.1007/s10548-021-00847-z.

Wolfram, T. (2023). (Not just) Intelligence stratifies the occupational hierarchy: Ranking 360 professions by IQ and non-cognitive traits. *Intelligence*, *98*, 101755. https://doi.org/10.1016/j.intell.2023.101755.

Wu, H., Guo, Y., Yang, Y., Zhao, L., & Guo, C. (2021). A meta-analysis of the longitudinal relationship between academic self-concept and academic achievement. *Educational Psychology Review, 33*, 1749–1778. https://doi.org/10.1007/s10648-021-09600-1.

Wynn, K. (1990). Children's understanding of counting. *Cognition, 36*, 155–193. http://doi.org/10.1016/0010-0277(90)90003-3.

Yarkoni, T., Speer, N. K., Balota, D. A., McAvoy, M. P., & Zacks, J. M. (2008). Pictures of a thousand words: Investigating the neural mechanisms of reading with extremely rapid event-related fMRI. *NeuroImage, 42*(2), 973–987. https://doi.org/10.1016/j.neuroimage.2008.04.258.

Yeatman, J. D., Dougherty, R. F., Ben-Shachar, M., & Wandell, B. A. (2012). Development of white matter and reading skills. *Proceedings of the National Academy of Sciences of the United States of America, 109*(44), E3045–E3053. https://doi.org/10.1073/pnas.1206792109.

Yeo, B. T., Krienen, F. M., Sepulcre, J. et al. (2011). The organization of the human cerebral cortex estimated by intrinsic functional connectivity. *Journal of Neurophysiology, 106*(1), 1125–1165. https://doi.org/10.1152/jn.00338.2011.

Yeo, D. J., Pollack, C., Merkley, R., Ansari, D., & Price, G. R. (2020). The "inferior temporal numeral area" distinguishes numerals from other character categories during passive viewing: A representational similarity analysis. *NeuroImage, 214*, 116716. https://doi.org/10.1016/j.neuroimage.2020.116716.

Yeshurun, Y., Nguyen, M., & Hasson, U. (2021). The default mode network: Where the idiosyncratic self meets the shared social world. *Nature Reviews Neuroscience, 22*(3), 181–192. https://doi.org/10.1038/s41583-020-00420-w.

Yi, H., Xiao, M., Chen, X. et al. (2023). Resting-state functional network connectivity underlying conscientiousness in school-aged children. *Child Neuropsychology*, 1–17. https://doi.org/10.1080/09297049.2023.2221757.

Young, C. B., Wu, S. S., & Menon, V. (2012). The neurodevelopmental basis of math anxiety. *Psychological Science, 23*(5), 492–501. https://doi.org/10.1177/0956797611429134.

Zatorre, R. J., Fields, R. D., & Johansen-Berg, H. (2012). Plasticity in gray and white: Neuroimaging changes in brain structure during learning. *Nature Neuroscience, 15*(4), 528–536. https://doi.org/10.1038/nn.3045.

Zeithamova, D., Mack, M. L., Braunlich, K. et al. (2019). Brain mechanisms of concept learning. *Journal of Neuroscience, 39*(42), 8259–8266. https://doi.org/10.1523/JNEUROSCI.1166-19.2019.

Zhang, L., Kirschner, P. A., Cobern, W. W., & Sweller, J. (2022). There is an evidence crisis in science educational policy. *Educational Psychology Review, 34*(2), 1157–1176. https://doi.org/10.1007/s10648-021-09646-1.

Zippert, E. L., & Rittle-Johnson, B. (2020). The home math environment: More than numeracy. *Early Childhood Research Quarterly, 50*(3), 4–15. https://doi.org/10.1016/j.ecresq.2018.07.009.

Zorzi, M., Priftis, K., & Umiltà, C. (2002). Neglect disrupts the mental number line. *Nature, 417*, 138–139. https://doi.org/10.1038/417138a.

# Cambridge Elements ☰

## Applied Evolutionary Science

### David F. Bjorklund
*Florida Atlantic University*

David F. Bjorklund is a Professor of Psychology at Florida Atlantic University in Boca Raton, Florida. He is the Editor-in-Chief of the *Journal of Experimental Child Psychology*, the Vice President of the Evolution Institute, and has written numerous articles and books on evolutionary developmental psychology, with a particular interest in the role of immaturity in evolution and development.

### About the Series

This series presents original, concise, and authoritative reviews of key topics in applied evolutionary science. Highlighting how an evolutionary approach can be applied to real-world social issues, many Elements in this series will include findings from programs that have produced positive educational, social, economic, or behavioral benefits. Cambridge Elements in Applied Evolutionary Science is published in association with the Evolution Institute.

 THE EVOLUTION INSTITUTE

# Cambridge Elements ☰

## Applied Evolutionary Science

Printed in the United States
by Baker & Taylor Publisher Services